A SKETCH-MAP HISTORY OF THE GREAT WAR AND AFTER

A SKETCH-MAP HISTORY
OF THE
GREAT WAR AND AFTER
1914—1935

BY

IRENE RICHARDS B.A.
HISTORY DEPARTMENT LATYMER SCHOOL EDMONTON LONDON

J. B. GOODSON B.A. F.R.G.S.
GEOGRAPHY DEPARTMENT LATYMER SCHOOL EDMONTON LONDON

AND

J. A. MORRIS B.Sc.(ECON.)
GEOGRAPHY DEPARTMENT LATYMER SCHOOL EDMONTON LONDON

GEORGE G. HARRAP & COMPANY LTD.
LONDON   TORONTO   BOMBAY   SYDNEY

First published 1938
by GEORGE G. HARRAP & CO. LTD.
182 *High Holborn, London, W.C.*1

Made in Great Britain.   Printed by Turnbull & Spears, Edinburgh

PREFACE

THE kind reception given to the two previous volumes of sketch-map histories of Britain and Europe up to the Great War has encouraged us to continue the story after 1914 to bring the subject-matter up to the present time. The present volume includes a few maps and notes on the causes of the War, and thus overlaps to a certain extent the preceding volumes because it seems desirable to preface the story of the War with some outline of its origins. This volume has not been divided into two sections, British and European, for it has been found impossible to treat the War-campaigns of Britain apart from those of her Allies. The part played by Britain, however, has received fuller treatment.

The work of writing the book and designing the maps has provided its three authors during the past few months with exercises of absorbing interest. There is no shortage of material for study, and the problems of discounting prejudice and reconciling conflicting points of view are difficulties which the history-teacher will not find insuperable. The authors have kept in mind, however, the point of view of the history-student. An inquiry in any secondary-school upper form will reveal a new generation that knows neither Passchendaele nor Verdun. How is this mass of new material, unfamiliar names, and strange ideas to be assimilated by the adolescent pupil? The task will doubtless be difficult, but not impossible, for our pupils have a very lively interest in the problems of post-War Europe.

The first step, as we see it, is to get the pupil familiar with the new topographic detail—he must know the map of Europe thoroughly so that names, e.g., the Marne and Vistula, Lemberg and Nish, are something more than mere names applied to rivers, towns, and battles. The second problem is to train the pupil to use this knowledge of position as a base on which to build up his framework of historical knowledge. No better method of doing this can be devised than to require him to draw for himself sketch-maps or diagrams which will synthesize the whole of what he knows which bears upon any particular problem.

The book contains many examples of this type of summary-map. They are merely suggestive of what can be done. Many of them have been used in class already. Experiment has shown that pupils can work from a map (using it without the text) and from it construct notes of the principal ideas. The more valuable exercise, however, is to make one's own sketches, and pupils should be encouraged to do this from the start, using the examples in the book only as guides and modifying them wherever possible. The more useful the alterations that a pupil can make in any map, the better is the quality of his study likely to be.

This sketch-map history, like its predecessors, owes its inspiration and accomplishment to the happy relations which exist between the history and geography departments of the Latymer School, Edmonton. Our thanks are due to many of our colleagues for helpful hints and suggestions and for revising the proofs ; and to our general editor, Mr George Taylor, for valuable criticisms at all stages of the work.

Suggestions for the improvement of this sketch-map history will be gratefully received.

IRENE RICHARDS
J. B. GOODSON
J. A. MORRIS

LATYMER SCHOOL
EDMONTON, N.9

CONTENTS

THE ORIGINS OF THE WAR

THE GREAT WAR (1914–1918)

THE PEACE CONFERENCE OF PARIS (1919)

CONTENTS

THE ORIGINS OF THE WAR

The Spark—the Sarajevo Murders

On Sunday, June 28, 1914, Franz Ferdinand, Archduke of Austria, and his wife paid an official visit to Sarajevo, the capital of Bosnia. As the royal visitors entered the town, a bomb was thrown at their car by a Bosnian student and exploded near to them. An hour after this narrow escape they were shot dead by another Bosnian student. This assassination of these two members of the Austrian royal family precipitated the world's greatest war.

The Powder—the Condition of Europe in 1914

For many years before 1914 Europe had been drifting towards war. On several occasions in the previous decade war had seemed imminent, but the catastrophe had been averted (see Map 4 and notes on p. 14.) Europe in 1914 was like a powder-magazine, and what is remarkable is not that it exploded, but that the event was delayed so long.

The Underlying Causes of the Great War

I. AUSTRIA AND PAN-SLAVISM

MAP I

The most disturbing force in Europe was the idea of nationalism. Its rapid growth in Austria-Hungary and Turkey was leading to the disruption of two ancient empires. Refusing to give way to the demands of the peoples within the Empire, Austrian statesmen sought to extend their rule over other non-German peoples. They wanted to dominate the Serbs; in so doing they encountered the firm opposition of the Slav people, who were inspired by propaganda for Pan-Slavism—the demand for unity of Slav people within a Slav state.

ANGLO-GERMAN RIVALRY IN AFRICA

The Cape-to-Cairo project and the German plan of a united German Central Africa.

II. GERMAN IMPERIALISM INVOLVING RIVALRY WITH BRITAIN

After 1890 the control of Germany's affairs passed into the hands of Kaiser William II, who aroused distrust and alarm by his warlike utterances. Bismarck had regarded Germany as a " satiated state," but the Kaiser had a vision of his empire as the dominant world power. German philosophers taught the superiority of the German nation over others. Treitschke maintained that only by war could his nation gain the supremacy that nature intended for her. Other writers conceived the plan of uniting all the Germans in one powerful state. This was the doctrine of Pan-Germanism.

This vigorous patriotism found expression in Germany's demand for 'a place

MAP 2

THE ARMED CAMP

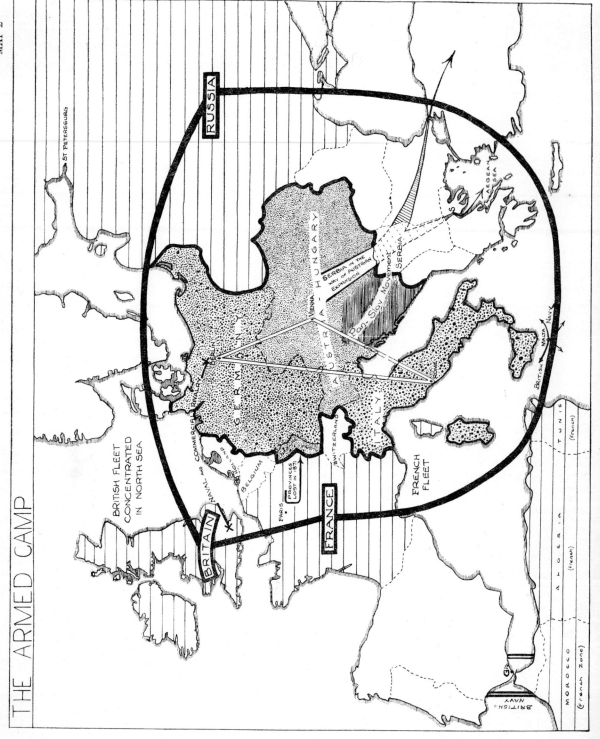

RUSSIA

ST PETERSBURG

GERMANY

AUSTRIA - HUNGARY

VIENNA

SERBIA in the way of Austrian Expansion

Pan-Slav Movement

SERBIA

AEGEAN SEA

BRITISH FLEET CONCENTRATED IN NORTH SEA

NAVAL AND COMMERCIAL RIVALRY

HOLLAND

BELGIUM

SWITZERLAND

ITALY

MALTA Navy

British Navy

BRITAIN

PARIS

PROVINCES LOST IN 1871

FRANCE

FRENCH FLEET

TUNIS (French)

ALGERIA (French)

MOROCCO (French Zone)

BRITISH NAVY

in the sun.' Colonies were desired by the German merchants, too, who wanted new markets for their goods. To protect German colonies a great navy was constructed. Such a policy aroused the fears of Great Britain—Germany's chief competitor in the markets and carrying-trade of the world, and the imperial power which had secured the largest and most desirable share of the colonial spoils.

III. RIVALRY BETWEEN RUSSIA AND THE CENTRAL POWERS

Weakened in the Far East by her failure in the Russo-Japanese War (1904–1905), Russia revived her interest in the Near East. Her ambition to dominate the Balkans and to control the Straits brought her into conflict with Austria and Germany. These powers had themselves hopes of expanding at the expense of Turkey.

Austria had concentrated her ambitions on the Balkans after the downfall of Hapsburg influence in Germany and Italy in 1866. Meanwhile the Germans had developed great commercial interests in Turkey and were constructing the Berlin-Bagdad railway ; the Kaiser posed as the friend and protector of the Sultan. The two Central Powers were united in opposition to Russia's schemes in the Near East.

IV. FRANCO-GERMAN SUSPICION

The bitterness of France towards Germany owing to the loss of Alsace-Lorraine in 1870 was a constant source of anxiety to German statesmen. Though the French nation by 1914 had almost ceased to hope for a restoration of these provinces, the rulers of Germany still felt that France was waiting for an opportunity for revenge ; the race in armaments increased this fear of insecurity.

V. MILITARISM

Great armies appeared in Europe for the first time after the middle of the nineteenth century. The development of industry and communications made possible the equipment and transport of vast armies and the mobilization of the entire nation.

After the Franco-Prussian War (1870–1871), Germany and France introduced universal conscription and the maintenance of a great standing army. The race in armaments had begun. Then, urged by von Tirpitz, the Kaiser commenced his ' Great Navy ' policy, and a fierce competition of dreadnought-building sprang up between Great Britain and Germany. Attempts were made to check the wasteful and dangerous growth of European armaments at the two Hague Conferences of 1899 and 1907. These conferences failed, the Kaiser being mainly responsible for their failure.

In Germany and Austria the military authorities became all too influential, and in the crisis of 1914 they overruled the statesmen.

VI. THE ARMED CAMP

One of the most striking characteristics of pre-War Europe was its division into two rival alliances of opposing powers. These alliances, though defensive in aim, created suspicion and uneasiness and led to the piling up of armaments. Moreover, a quarrel between any two states involved the rest ; the dispute between Russia and Austria tended to bring about a dispute between France and Germany.

(a) The Triple Alliance—Austria, Germany, Italy

This grouping began in 1879 as a *Dual Alliance* between Austria and Germany. Since 1870 Bismarck, the German Chancellor, had feared that France, bitter over the loss of Alsace-Lorraine, would plan a war of revenge. He did not fear France alone, but he did fear France in combination with any other great power. The Dual Alliance of 1879 provided for mutual defence in case of attack from Russia. On the French seizure of Tunis in 1881, Italy became a partner in this defensive pact, and in 1882 the Triple Alliance was concluded. Italy was not a whole-hearted ally ; she was unwilling to oppose Great Britain and France, whose fleets dominated the Mediterranean, and she nursed a grievance against Austria, who retained in Trentino part of ' Italia Irredenta.'

(b) The Triple Entente—France, Russia, Great Britain

• This rival group of powers arose in mutual fear of the Central European alliances.

(i) *The Dual Alliance of* 1894.—After 1890 Russia and France found themselves isolated while Central Europe was united in the Triple Alliance. Overcoming a dislike of each other's form of government, they combined against their common rivals and made an alliance in 1894.

(ii) *Entente Cordiale* (1904).—For over thirty years Great Britain had endeavoured to avoid participation in continental alliances ; at the beginning of the twentieth century it appeared dangerous to remain friendless in Europe. Imperial issues, *e.g.*, over Egypt, had made her unfriendly to France ; for a century British statesmen had regarded Russia with alarm and distrust. The obvious ally for Great Britain appeared to be Germany, but the Kaiser had begun his ' Great Navy ' policy and refused to abandon it. This was a threat to the very existence of Great Britain, and it forced her into the arms of France. Imperial issues were amicably settled and the Entente Cordiale was arranged in 1904.

(iii) *Triple Entente* (1907).—An understanding prompted by France, their mutual friend, was soon realized by Great Britain and Russia, who were both increasingly suspicious of German designs. This agreement was concluded in 1907.

THE CRISES BEFORE 1914

After 1901, when Germany had finally rejected British overtures towards a better understanding and Britain drew away from a policy of ' splendid isolation ' to enter the European system of alliances, successive crises arose which heralded the approaching struggle. These ' incidents ' concerned Franco-German rivalry in North Africa and Russo-Austrian rivalry in the Balkans.

I. MOROCCO

Morocco was in a very disturbed condition, and France undertook to maintain order on the Algerian-Moroccan frontier. After the conclusion of the Entente Cordiale in 1904, Great Britain recognized the special interests of France in the country. The Kaiser, however, visited Tangiers in 1905 and, in a menacing speech, supported the independence of Morocco in order to safeguard German economic interests. He demanded that the question be settled at an international conference. French opposition to Germany nearly led to war, but they were not ready themselves and their ally, Russia, had just been crushingly defeated by Japan.

The conference met at Algeciras in 1906. Britain supported France firmly. The independence of Morocco was affirmed, but it was agreed that France should be responsible for keeping internal order.

In 1911 came a further crisis. France had landed troops and occupied the capital,

MAP 3

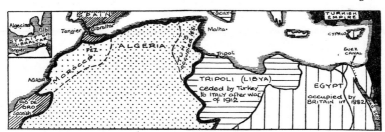

NORTH-WEST AFRICA: THE MOROCCAN QUESTION
Territory shown with dotted shading is under French control.

Fez, on the plea of maintaining order. Germany was suspicious and asserted the claim that there was a breach of the Algeciras treaty.

The crisis was acute. Germany dispatched a gunboat, the *Panther*, to Agadir to protect the interests of German subjects. Great Britain's warning to Germany and strong support to her ally forced Germany to modify her demands and checked her warlike attitude. In return for concessions in Central Africa, Germany acknowledged France's Protectorate in Morocco.

It was a diplomatic rebuff for Germany; her antagonism to England increased.

II. ARISING OUT OF THE EASTERN QUESTION

The chief storm-centre of Europe was the Turkish Empire, growing steadily weaker and forced to rely more and more upon Germany, the Sultan's new ally. The Kaiser had shown his interest in Turkey in 1898 by his visit to the Sultan, when all Europe was horrified at the news of the Turkish massacres of her Armenian subjects, and by his announcement to extend German protection to the Moslem peoples of the world. He had gained concessions for railway development under German direction—a prelude to his dream of a Berlin-Bagdad railway.

This *Drang Nach Osten* conflicted with the aspirations of the Balkan peoples who wished to take advantage of the difficulties of the Porte in their endeavour to secure independence.

(a) The Bosnian Crisis of 1908

In 1908 Austria annexed Bosnia and Herzegovina, two territories which she had administered since the Congress of Berlin (1878). These two provinces were largely inhabited by Serbs, and the action of Austria excited the indignation of the Slav peoples. The peace of Europe depended upon the attitude of Russia, to whom the Serbs naturally turned for assistance. Russia protested, but was compelled to submit

15

MAP 4

BALKAN CRISES

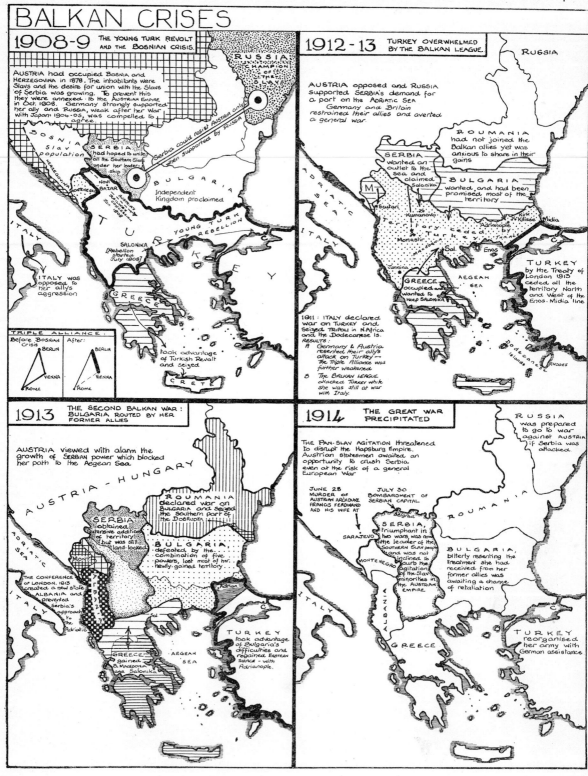

1908-9 — THE YOUNG TURK REVOLT AND THE BOSNIAN CRISIS

AUSTRIA had occupied BOSNIA and HERZEGOVINA in 1878. The inhabitants were Slavs and the desire for union with the Slavs of Serbia was growing. To prevent this they were annexed to the AUSTRIAN EMPIRE in Oct. 1908. Germany strongly supported her ally and Russia, weak after her War with Japan 1904-05, was compelled to agree.

RUSSIA CHAMPION of the SLAVS

BOSNIA Slav population

SERBIA had hoped to unite all the Southern Slavs under her leadership

Serbia could resist Austria only when supported by Russia

HERZEGOVINA

MONTENEGRO

NOVI BAZAR

BULGARIA — Independent Kingdom proclaimed

YOUNG TURK REBELLION

SALONIKA — Rebellion started July 1908

TURKEY

GREECE

ITALY was opposed to her ally's aggression

took advantage of Turkish Revolt and seized

CRETE

TRIPLE ALLIANCE:
Before Bosnian Crisis — BERLIN, VIENNA, ROME
After: — BERLIN, VIENNA, ROME

1912-13 — TURKEY OVERWHELMED BY THE BALKAN LEAGUE

RUSSIA

AUSTRIA opposed and RUSSIA supported SERBIA's demand for a port on the ADRIATIC SEA. Germany and Britain restrained their allies and averted a general war.

ROUMANIA had not joined the Balkan allies yet was anxious to share in their gains

SERBIA wanted an outlet to the sea and claimed Salonika

BULGARIA wanted, and had been promised most of the territory

ADRIATIC SEA

ITALY

Scutari

Kumanovo

Monastir

Territory ceded by Turkey

Kirk Kilisse — Adrianople — Midia

MACEDONIA

Janina

GREECE occupied and wanted to keep SALONIKA

Sal.

Enos

AEGEAN SEA

TURKEY by the Treaty of London 1913 ceded all the territory North and West of the Enos-Midia line

Dodecanese Islands

RHODES

1911: ITALY declared war on TURKEY and seized TRIPOLI in N.Africa and the Dodecanese Is.
RESULTS:
A Germany & Austria resented their ally's attack on Turkey — The Triple Alliance was further weakened
B The BALKAN LEAGUE attacked TURKEY while she was still at war with Italy.

1913 — THE SECOND BALKAN WAR: BULGARIA ROUTED BY HER FORMER ALLIES

AUSTRIA viewed with alarm the growth of SERBIAN power which blocked her path to the Aegean Sea

AUSTRIA - HUNGARY

ROUMANIA declared war on BULGARIA and seized the southern part of the Dobruja

SERBIA obtained extensive additions of territory but was still land-locked

BULGARIA defeated by the combination of five powers, lost most of her newly-gained territory

ADRIATIC SEA

MONTENEGRO

THE CONFERENCE of LONDON, 1913 created a new state ALBANIA and prevented Serbia's approach to the Adriatic

Adrian.

Sal.

GREECE gained S.Macedonia and Salonika

AEGEAN SEA

TURKEY took advantage of Bulgaria's difficulties and regained EASTERN THRACE - with Adrianople.

1914 — THE GREAT WAR PRECIPITATED

THE PAN-SLAV AGITATION threatened to disrupt the Hapsburg Empire. Austrian statesmen awaited an opportunity to crush Serbia even at the risk of a general European War

RUSSIA was prepared to go to war against AUSTRIA if Serbia was attacked

JUNE 28 MURDER OF AUSTRIAN ARCHDUKE FRANCIS FERDINAND AND HIS WIFE AT

JULY 30 BOMBARDMENT OF SERBIAN CAPITAL

Belgrade

SARAJEVO

SERBIA, triumphant in two wars, was now the leader of the Southern Slav people and was not inclined to curb the agitation of the Slav minorities in the AUSTRIAN EMPIRE

MONTENEGRO

ALBANIA

ITALY

GREECE

ROUMANIA

BULGARIA, bitterly resenting the treatment she had received from her former allies was awaiting a chance of retaliation

TURKEY reorganised her army with German assistance

when the Kaiser threatened armed support for Austria, for her military machine had not recovered from the Japanese War of 1904–1905.

(b) The Balkan Wars of 1912 and 1913

In 1911 Italy seized Tripoli, a Turkish province in Northern Africa, where for many years she had pursued a policy of economic penetration. War with Turkey followed. It ended in 1912 and left Turkey in an exhausted condition. Taking advantage of this weakness, Greece, Serbia, and Bulgaria formed a 'Balkan League,' which attacked and defeated Turkey.

This Balkan War of 1912 gravely threatened the interests of Germany and Austria, but the Great Powers were in agreement in wanting the war localized. A conference was summoned in London to settle the division of the territory which Turkey had been forced to surrender.

Map 4 shows the conflicting claims of the successful Balkan allies. Austria, supported by Germany, intervened to prevent Serbia from securing access to the sea through Albania. This was the second successful attempt by Austria to curb the Pan-Slav movement. War was averted only by the influence of Germany and Britain.

Serbia, however, was compensated by accessions of territory in Macedonia at the expense of Bulgaria, who objected and reopened the war, this time against her former allies and a new rival to the north—Roumania. Bulgaria was overwhelmingly defeated by the combination against her, and Serbia annexed large territories at her expense. This greatly enlarged and strengthened Serbia aroused the deep resentment of Austria. Only Germany's restraining influence and Italy's refusal to co-operate prevented an immediate attack. Instead, she waited for an opportunity when she would have a better excuse for intervention. She had not long to wait. A year later the heir to the Austrian throne was assassinated at Sarajevo.

THE CRISIS OF 1914

The Archduke Franz Ferdinand had favoured a policy of reconciliation with the Slavs within the Austrian Empire. Because of this attitude he was disliked by the ruling class in Vienna and by the Magyar statesmen of Hungary. The Slavs within the Empire, seeking union with the Serbs, their fellow Slavs, also opposed him.

Nevertheless, the Austrian Government seized the opportunity of his assassination to charge the Serbian Government with the responsibility.

Austria presented an ultimatum with demands which threatened the existence of Serbia as an independent state. The Austrian statesmen knew that war would almost certainly lead to a general European war and that the ruin of the Austrian Empire was inevitable if they were defeated. They took the risk.

The Emperor Francis Joseph first sought and obtained the assurance of support from the German Kaiser. Although Serbia accepted almost all the humiliating demands of this ultimatum, Austria treated the Serbian reply as a rejection and declared war on July 28.

1. EUROPE AT WAR

Germany was anxious to confine the war to Austria and Serbia, but Russia stood by Serbia. There were, however, no statesmen capable of controlling the situation;

B

Bethman-Hollweg, Chancellor of Germany, and Sir Edward Grey, the British Foreign Secretary, both attempted unsuccessfully to stay the hand of Austria. The Kaiser sent a twelve-hour ultimatum to Russia demanding a suspension of mobilization; this was not answered in time, and he declared war on Russia immediately. France stood by her ally, Russia, and declared war on Germany.

II. ATTITUDE OF GREAT BRITAIN

No one knew if Great Britain would support France and Russia. There was only friendship, not a military alliance binding the countries together. Sir Edward Grey asked both France and Germany if each would respect the neutrality of Belgium according to their treaty-obligations. Whereas France so promised, Germany demanded passage for her armies, and when the Belgians refused, Germany declared war on Belgium. The British line of action was now clear. Great Britain had promised by the Treaty of London (1839)—a promise repeated from time to time—to guarantee the neutrality of Belgium. Germany could not be tolerated in the Netherlands; wars had been fought against Louis XIV and against Napoleon to maintain their independence.

In a moving scene on August 4 in the House of Commons Sir Edward Grey announced the declaration of war against Germany.

REVIEW OF THE REASONS WHY THE GREAT POWERS WENT TO WAR

I. AUSTRIA-HUNGARY

(*a*) To crush the Pan-Slav movement, which made the task of controlling the Austrian Slavs more difficult.

(*b*) To dominate the Balkans and, by crushing Serbia, to control the route to the Ægean port of Salonika.

II. GERMANY

(*a*) To preserve her ally, Austria, from the consequences of the attack on Serbia.

(*b*) To maintain and extend Germany's prestige as a world power.

(*c*) To preserve German security; the Kaiser believed that there was a conspiracy among the powers of the Triple Entente to encircle and destroy Germany.

(*d*) To begin what was believed to be an inevitable war at a propitious time for Germany by a surprise attack. Britain seemed to be preoccupied with her own troubles in Ireland and India. The suffragette campaign seemed to demonstrate the weakness of the British Government.

III. RUSSIA

(*a*) To preserve Serbia from destruction.

(The Tsar, a weak but well-intentioned ruler, was isolated by the corrupt and inefficient system of government from a knowledge of the weakness of his country and so of the dreadful risks he was taking.)

(*b*) To pursue the long-cherished aims of dominating the Balkans and Constantinople.

(*c*) To strengthen her authority over a semi-rebellious state. The Russian ministers believed that a victorious war would be the best bulwark against revolution.

IV. FRANCE

(*a*) To fulfil treaty obligations with Russia. She feared for her own safety if Russia were beaten.

(*b*) To combat the growing militarism of Germany.

V. GREAT BRITAIN

(*a*) To fulfil treaty-obligations to Belgium.

(*b*) To support France ; a naval agreement had been reached whereby France kept her fleet in the Mediterranean, while Britain protected the Channel coasts.

(*c*) To preserve her security threatened by (i) German domination of the Netherlands, (ii) the growth of the German navy, (iii) a vital disturbance of the ' balance of power.' If Germany overran the Continent, Great Britain would have been menaced by a great peril.

MAP 5

WESTERN FRONT

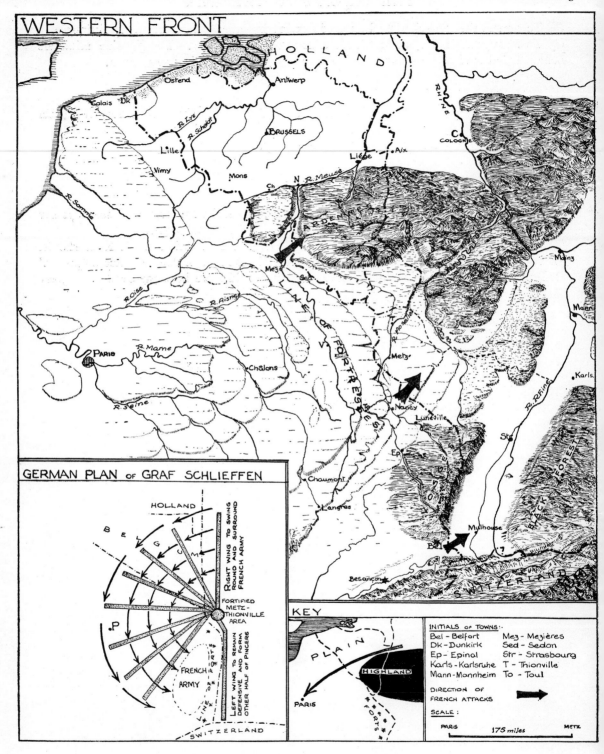

HOLLAND

Ostend

Antwerp

Calais ˙Dk

R.Lys

R.Scheldt

BRUSSELS

Liège ˙Aix

RHINE

COLOGNE

C

L'Ille

Vimy

Mons

Ch N R.Meuse

ARDENNES

Mainz

R.Somme

Mez

Sed

R.Oise

R.Aisne

LINE OF FORTRESSES

Rhine

Mann

PARIS

R.Marne

Châlons

Metz

Mann

R.Seine

Nancy

Lunéville

Karls.

Str

Chaumont

Ep

Langres

Mulhouse

BLACK FOREST

Bel

Besançon

SWITZERLAND

GERMAN PLAN of GRAF SCHLIEFFEN

HOLLAND

B E L G I U M

FORTIFIED
METZ -
THIONVILLE
AREA

RIGHT WING TO SWING
ROUND AND SURROUND
FRENCH ARMY

˙P

FRENCH
ARMY

LEFT WING TO REMAIN
DEFENSIVE AND FORM
OTHER HALF OF PINCERS

SWITZERLAND

KEY

PLAIN

HIGHLAND

PARIS

FORTS

INITIALS of TOWNS:-
Bel - Belfort   Mez - Mezières
Dk - Dunkirk   Sed - Sedon
Ep - Epinal   Str - Strasbourg
Karls - Karlsruhe   T - Thionville
Mann - Mannheim   To - Toul

DIRECTION OF
FRENCH ATTACKS

SCALE:

PARIS   175 miles   METZ

THE GREAT WAR (1914–1918)

MILITARY PLANS IN 1914

ON the declaration of war the French and German military staffs immediately proceeded to put into action plans which they had long prepared and, in theory, perfected.

I. THE GERMAN PLAN : TO PARIS *via* BELGIUM

Realizing the inferior nature of the Russian military machine, the German Imperial Staff had decided that a small force would suffice to defend the eastern frontier. They believed that France could speedily be paralysed by a lightning attack delivered by the full weight of the German armies. On the collapse of France the victorious troops could be transferred to the east and Russia overwhelmed.

This lightning stroke could not be directed against the eastern frontier of France, for the line from Belgium to Switzerland presented the following obstacles :
(*a*) The Ardennes—wooded upland with poor communications.
(*b*) A line of fortresses from Mezières to Epinal.
(*c*) The almost impregnable Vosges Mountains.
(*d*) The Gate of Burgundy, guarded by the fortress of Belfort.

An attack through the Belgian plain alone offered hopes of immediate success ; the chief defect of such a plan was political, not military. It involved the violation of the neutrality of Belgium, contrary to treaty-obligations, and might entail the intervention of Great Britain. Nevertheless, this was the plan adopted and worked out as early as 1905 by Schlieffen, then the head of the German military staff.

II. SCHLIEFFEN'S PLAN

The left wing from Metz to the Swiss frontier was to stand on the defensive and, if necessary, retire. The right wing was to be made six times as strong and was to swing irresistibly through the plains, occupy Paris, and drive the French army in disorder against the high land in the east of France. In 1914 Schlieffen's successor, Moltke, put the plan into execution, and thus drew the weight of Belgium and Britain against him. It was the small armies of these two states which turned the scale and brought about the failure of the plan.

III. THE FRENCH PLAN

Fortifications and nature combined to make eastern France ideal for defence, but the French were so infatuated with the idea that ' attack is the best defence ' that they proposed to undertake two invasions of Germany. In 1914 Germany sprang a surprise by the number of men massed in the first assault. As a result the French advances were soon brought to a standstill, and in Lorraine their troops were thrust back to their own advantage upon the line of fortresses.

Britain maintained a small but very efficient army of about 160,000 men, and on the outbreak of war, over half of these, with all necessary supplies, were immediately

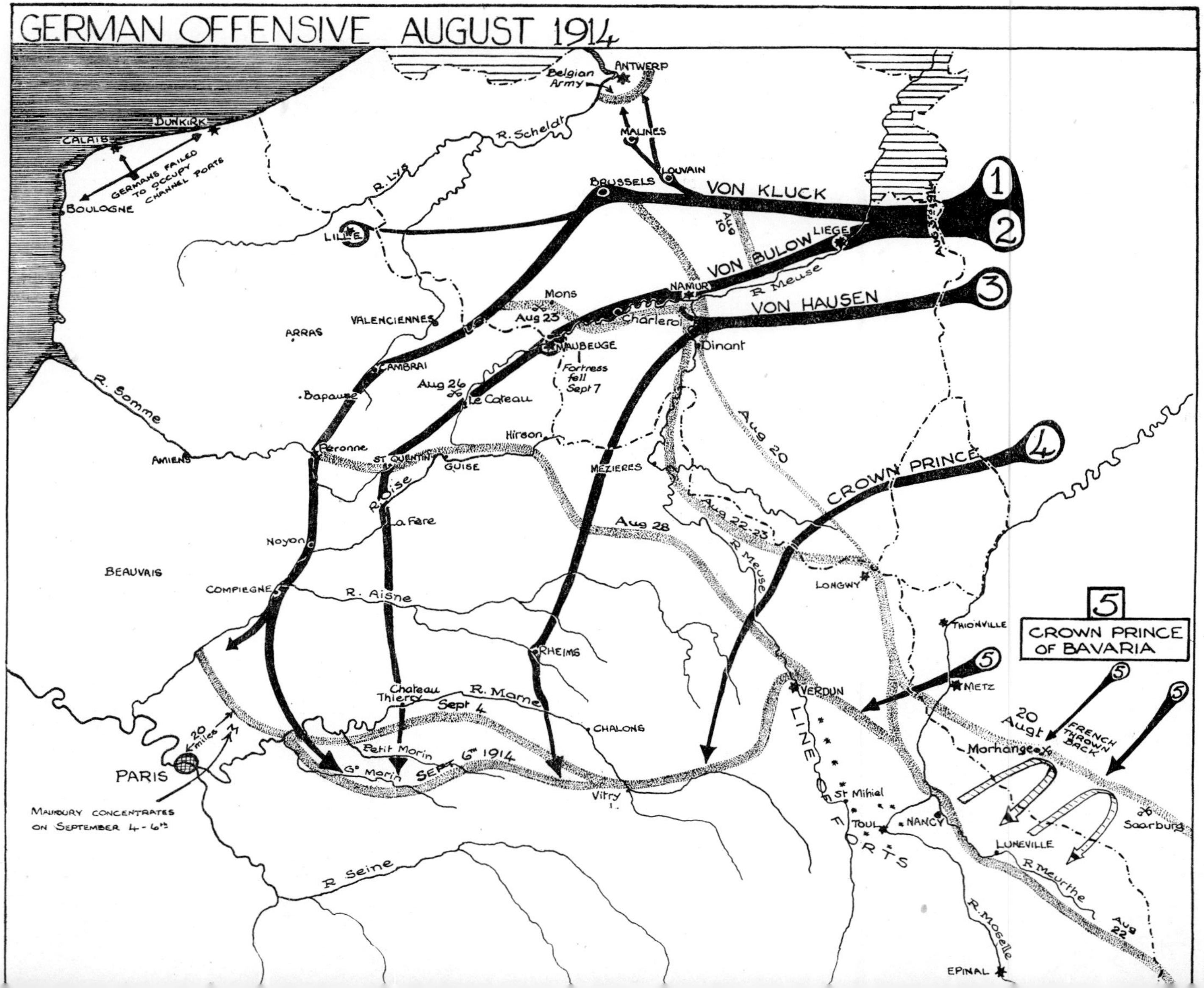

MAP 6

GERMAN OFFENSIVE AUGUST 1914

CALAIS

DUNKIRK

GERMANS FAILED TO OCCUPY PORTS

BOULOGNE

R. Yser

ANTWERP

Belgian Army

R. Scheldt

MALINES

LOUVAIN

BRUSSELS

LIEGE

Aug 20

NAMUR

Aug 5

R. Meuse

Dinant

Charleroi

VON KLUCK 1 2

VON BULOW 3

VON HAUSEN

LILLE

VALENCIENNES

ARRAS

Mons

Aug 23

MAUBEUGE

Fortress fell Sept 7

R. Sambre

CAMBRAI

Aug 26

Le Cateau

Hirson

MEZIERES

Aug 28

R. Meuse

Aug 22-23

R. Somme

AMIENS

BEAUVAIS

Bapaume

Peronne

St QUENTIN

La Fere

GUISE

OISE

Noyon

COMPIEGNE

R. Aisne

CROWN PRINCE

Aug 20

Longwy

THIONVILLE

METZ

VERDUN

LINE OF FORTS

St MIHIEL

TOUL

NANCY

R. Meurthe

LUNEVILLE

Aug 22

Saarburg

EPINAL

R. Moselle

20 Aug

Morhange

FRENCH THROWN BACK

5

CROWN PRINCE OF BAVARIA

5

5

5

RHEIMS

CHALONS

Vitry

R. Marne

Château Thierry

Sept 4

Petit Morin

Gd Morin

Sept 6th 1914

SEINE

R. Seine

PARIS

20 miles

MAUNOURY CONCENTRATES ON SEPTEMBER 4-6th

dispatched to the assistance of France. They first came into contact with the enemy near Mons, where they formed the left flank of the Allied line.

The German Offensive

Backed by excellent railways and working methodically to a time-table, the German armies of the right wing advanced against Liège, the fortress which guarded the gap between the Dutch frontier and the Ardennes country. They occupied the town on August 7, and the Belgian army fell back on Antwerp, where it served to detach considerable German forces and remained a thorn in the side of the main German advance. The German First Army, under Kluck, now swept over half Belgium and occupied the capital, Brussels. As soon as the Germans entered Belgium, the French Fifth Army advanced into the Ardennes from Mezières, hoping to outflank the German right wing. The extensive deployment of German troops in the west made this impossible, and, in fact, it was the French army which was in danger of being outflanked. The British Expeditionary Force came into line on the French left and helped to ward off this danger. The British first encountered Kluck's army at Mons and were forced to retreat. The Battle of Le Cateau was a rearguard action to cover this retirement.

On September 2, when his army had reached Compiègne, Kluck felt that the time had come for the decisive action. He swung his right wing inward to roll up the Allied left wing, and in doing so prematurely, he exposed his own lengthening line of communications to a counter-attack from the west. Galliéni, the Governor of Paris, immediately prepared to attack the German right wing, and the invaders were arrested and turned back after they had been within seventeen miles of Paris. On September 1 the Allied position had looked so unfavourable that the French Commander, Joffre, contemplated a general retirement to a line south of the River Seine; yet by September 17 the Germans instead had retreated northward to the River Aisne.

The Battle of the Marne (1914)

This spectacular reversal of fortunes is known as the Battle of the Marne. It was a decisive turning-point in the War. During the succeeding four years the Germans scored many successes, but nothing could offset the failure to secure victory in their original 'five-week campaign.' Thereafter time was on the side of the Allies, and the Germans suffered continuous and increasing pressure from the British blockade until their physical and moral resources were destroyed.

Causes of German Retreat

How the triumphal advance of the Germans was brought to a halt and turned into a retreat was as follows. The vital German right wing had been weakened by the withdrawal of troops to invest the fortresses of Antwerp and Mauberge and to reinforce the army on the Russian front. The transport of food-supplies had failed to keep up with the rapid advance of the German troops; field-kitchens had been left behind, and the soldiers were hungry as well as tired. The German High Command lost touch with the army commanders and, at one time, did not know the whereabouts of Kluck. The fortresses of Lorraine enabled Joffre to withdraw French troops from that sector

MAP 7

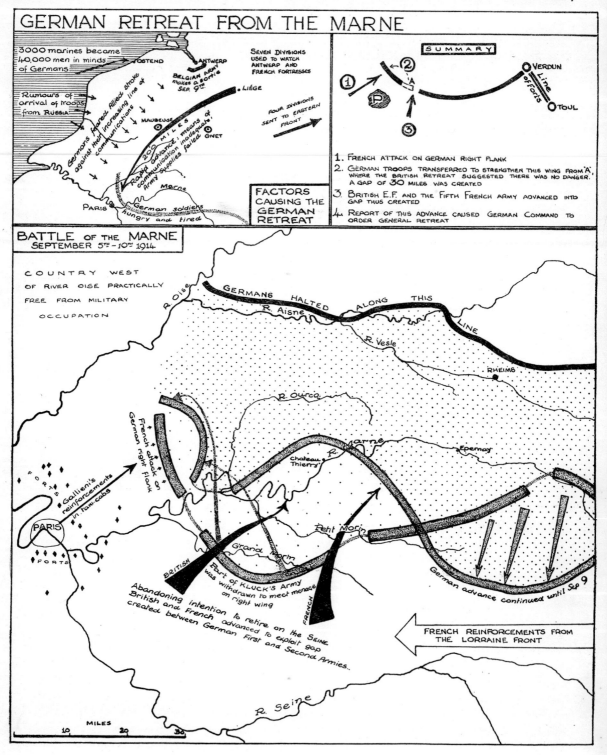

GERMAN RETREAT FROM THE MARNE

3000 marines became 40,000 men in minds of Germans

Rumours of arrival of troops from Russia

Germans feared Allied strike against their increasing line of communications

ANTWERP
OSTEND
BELGIAN ARMY makes a sortie SEP. 9TH
LIÉGE

MAUBEUGE
200 MILES
GIVET
Rapid advance; means of communication inadequate; Army communication supplies failed

Marne

PARIS

German soldiers hungry and tired

SEVEN DIVISIONS USED TO WATCH ANTWERP AND FRENCH FORTRESSES

FOUR DIVISIONS SENT TO EASTERN FRONT

FACTORS CAUSING THE GERMAN RETREAT

SUMMARY

VERDUN
TOUL
Line of forts

1. FRENCH ATTACK ON GERMAN RIGHT FLANK
2. GERMAN TROOPS TRANSFERRED TO STRENGTHEN THIS WING FROM 'A', WHERE THE BRITISH RETREAT SUGGESTED THERE WAS NO DANGER. A GAP OF 30 MILES WAS CREATED
3. BRITISH E.F. AND THE FIFTH FRENCH ARMY ADVANCED INTO GAP THUS CREATED
4. REPORT OF THIS ADVANCE CAUSED GERMAN COMMAND TO ORDER GENERAL RETREAT

BATTLE OF THE MARNE
SEPTEMBER 5TH – 10TH 1914

COUNTRY WEST OF RIVER OISE PRACTICALLY FREE FROM MILITARY OCCUPATION

R. OISE
GERMANS HALTED ALONG THIS LINE
R. Aisne
R. Vesle
RHEIMS

R. Ourcq
Marne
Chateau Thierry
Epernay

French attack on German right flank

Gallieni's reinforcements in taxi-cabs

NORTH

PARIS
FORTS

BRITISH

Grand Morin
Petit Morin

Part of KLUCK'S Army was withdrawn to meet menace on right wing

FRENCH

Abandoning intention to retire on the Seine British and French advanced to exploit gap created between German First and Second Armies.

German advance continued until Sep 9

FRENCH REINFORCEMENTS FROM THE LORRAINE FRONT

R. Seine

MILES
10   20   30

to form a new army—the Sixth—on the left wing. This force was directed by Galliéni against the exposed German right flank. This operation was hastened by the use of Parisian taxi-cabs to transport troops. Kluck successfully countered this threat by transferring to his right flank that part of his army which had reached the Grand Morin, where the rapid retreat of the B.E.F. suggested there was no danger. This, however, created a gap of thirty miles between the German First and Second Armies, and the B.E.F. and the French Fifth Army turned and advanced into the gap. The news of this Allied movement caused dismay in the German headquarters, where extreme nervousness already prevailed on account of their lengthened lines of communication. Accordingly, although their troops had suffered no important reverse, the High Command gave orders for a general retirement, which only came to an end at the line of the River Aisne.

THE EASTERN FRONT (1914)

I. THE GERMAN PLAN

As we have seen, this was to allot the minimum of forces to this front, and later to transfer the victorious western armies there after the defeat of France.

II. THE AUSTRIAN PLAN

The Austrian Commander shared the German view that Russian mobilization would take some time, but wished to take advantage of this by beginning an offensive immediately. His plan was to invade Poland from the south, and he expected, with the help of a German attack from the north, to cut off the Russian army in western Poland.

The Austrian scheme was frustrated by the surprising swiftness with which Russia carried out her mobilization.

III. THE RUSSIAN PLAN

At the outset the Russian Command desired to concentrate against Austria, and they planned to attack the province of Galicia simultaneously from the north and east. It was only to relieve the pressure on their ally, France, that they undertook in addition an immediate offensive against East Prussia. For this campaign they were ill prepared, but they succeeded in drawing German troops away from the western front at the crucial moment of the Battle of the Marne.

IV. THE CAMPAIGN IN GALICIA : THE BATTLE OF LEMBERG

The Austrian force marching northward from Galicia encountered and came near to surrounding the Russian army opposing it. In the meantime, however, the weaker Austrian army, facing eastward, was attacked near Lemberg by a greatly superior force and collapsed. This threatened the rear of the Austrian First Army, which was forced to retire when on the threshold of success. The two Austrian forces backed into each other and retreated in confusion some 150 miles to the River Dunajec. They abandoned the province of Galicia with the valuable Lemburg oil-wells and lost 350,000 men.

MAP 8

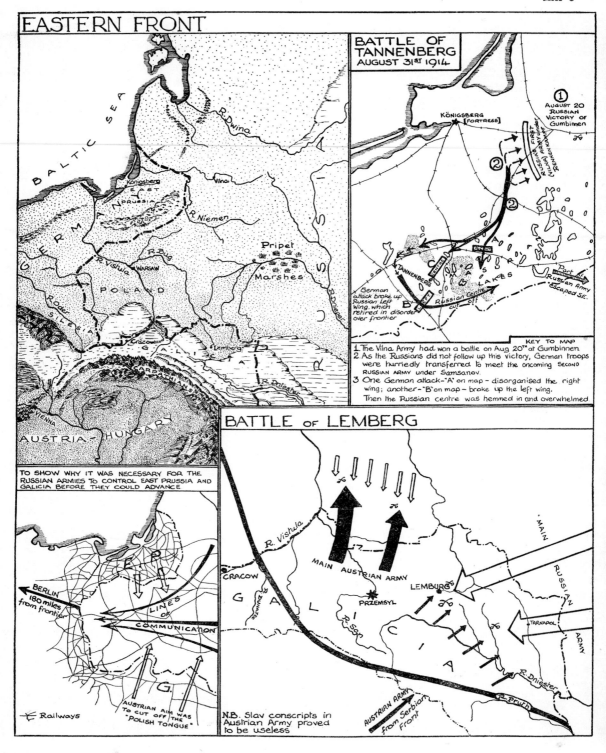

EASTERN FRONT

BALTIC SEA

R. Dwina

Königsberg
EAST
PRUSSIA
G E R M A N Y

Vilna

R. Niemen

R. Vistula

WARSAW
POLAND
R. Bug

Pripet
Marshes

R U S S I A

R. Dnieper

SILESIA

R. Oder

Cracow

Lemberg

G A L I C I A

R. Dniester

CARPATHIANS

VIENNA

AUSTRIA-HUNGARY

BATTLE OF TANNENBERG
AUGUST 31ST 1914

KÖNIGSBERG [FORTRESS]

① AUGUST 20 RUSSIAN VICTORY OF GUMBINNEN

②

②

RUSSIAN FIRST (VILNA) ARMY under RENNENKAMPF

TANNENBERG

"A"

Russian Centre cut off

"B"

MASURIAN LAKES

Part of Russian Army escaped S.E.

German attack broke up Russian left wing, which retired in disorder over frontier

KEY TO MAP

1. The Vilna Army had won a battle on Aug 20th at Gumbinnen.
2. As the Russians did not follow up this victory, German troops were hurriedly transferred to meet the oncoming SECOND RUSSIAN ARMY under Samsonov.
3. One German attack—"A" on map—disorganised the right wing; another—"B" on map—broke up the left wing.

Then the Russian centre was hemmed in and overwhelmed.

TO SHOW WHY IT WAS NECESSARY FOR THE RUSSIAN ARMIES TO CONTROL EAST PRUSSIA AND GALICIA BEFORE THEY COULD ADVANCE

E. P.

BERLIN 180 miles from frontier

LINES OF COMMUNICATION

G.

AUSTRIAN AIM WAS TO CUT OFF THE "POLISH TONGUE"

⌐ Railways

BATTLE of LEMBERG

R. Vistula

CRACOW

G A L I C I A

PRZEMYSL

R. San

MAIN AUSTRIAN ARMY

LEMBURG

MAIN

RUSSIAN ARMY

TARNOPOL

R. Dniester

AUSTRIAN ARMY from Serbian Front

R. Pruth

N.B. Slav conscripts in Austrian Army proved to be useless

V. THE CAMPAIGN IN EAST PRUSSIA : TANNENBERG

One Russian army attacked East Prussia from the direction of Vilna. It scored a minor victory near the frontier but failed to follow it up. A second Russian army approached East Prussia from the south, and its unexpectedly early arrival so alarmed the German commander that he prepared to withdraw behind the Vistula. A new commander, General Ludendorff,[1] was thereupon appointed, and thanks partly to the brilliant plan which he put into execution and partly to the folly of the Russians, Germany was able to secure at Tannenberg the greatest military triumph of the War.

Aided by their network of railways, the Germans massed their entire East Prussian forces against the Russian Second Army in the south. They drove back its flanks, surrounded its centre, and captured 90,000 prisoners.

The following facts contributed to the defeat of the Russians :

(*a*) Contact between the two Russian armies was interrupted by the Masurian lakes, forests, and marshes.

(*b*) There was serious enmity between the two Russian commanders.

(*c*) The lethargy of the Vilna army permitted the German forces opposing it to get away unhindered and to concentrate against the Russian Second Army under Samsonov.

(*d*) The speed with which Samsonov had been hurried to the attack over difficult sandy roads took him too far from his base and left his soldiers exhausted.

(*e*) Internal lines and good communications permitted the necessary rapid movement of German troops.

After Tannenberg the German troops turned eastward and expelled the Vilna army. The German advance was brought to an end only by the need to send assistance to the Austrians in Galicia.

NAVAL POWER (1914)

In 1914 the German navy was more powerful than the combined French and Russian fleets, but the entry of Great Britain into the War gave the Allies a great preponderance of sea-power.

By a fortunate chance the British navy was assembled at Portland for a practice mobilization in July, 1914. When war became imminent the fleet was ordered not to disperse and thus was prepared to exercise its superiority as soon as hostilities began. As a result the German navy stayed in port behind its impregnable coastal defences, and German overseas trade had to be abandoned immediately. A virtual blockade of the North Sea was instituted and all ships were stopped by search-parties from British warships. Germany had to rely upon foreign supplies reaching her circuitously *via* neutral countries.

On the other hand Allied shipping was hardly interrupted. There were a few German warships on the high seas when war broke out, and these attacked the principal trade-routes. The damage they did, however, was relatively slight, and the German raiders were practically all destroyed by December 8, 1914.

Thereafter the Allies were free to transport men and munitions to every theatre of war and to draw freely upon foreign food-supplies. Moreover, this freedom of movement was denied to the Central Powers, and by 1918 they suffered such shortage of vital raw materials and foodstuffs that they were unable to continue the War.

[1] With Hindenburg as his nominal chief.

MAP 9

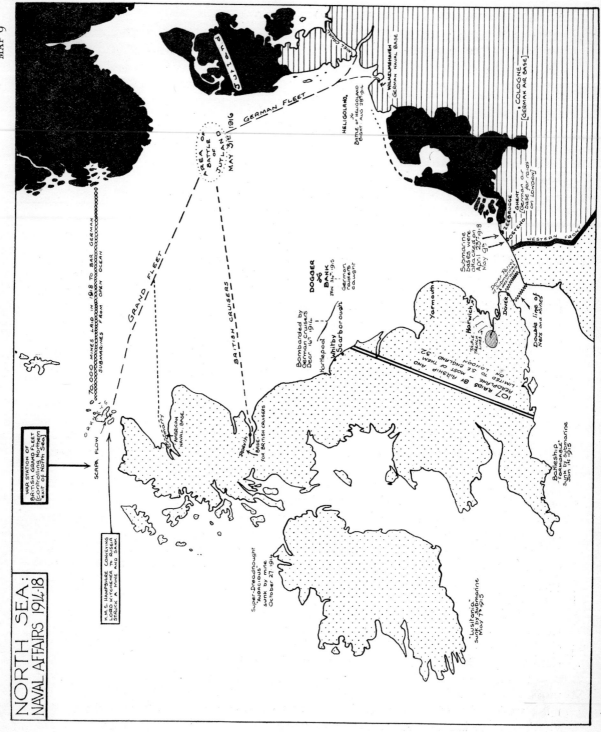

NORTH SEA: NAVAL AFFAIRS 1914-18

The situation on the seas was so favourable to the Allies that Jellicoe, the British Admiral, adopted a policy of extreme caution, refusing to risk losing these advantages for even a probable naval victory. Clearly any defeat of the British navy would have reversed the tables, for Britain could be starved out in a few weeks. Jellicoe was the only man " who could lose the war in an afternoon," and he therefore abandoned the Nelsonian tradition of seeking out the enemy and forcing him to give battle. The chief events in the North Sea during the early months of the War were as follows :

(*a*) The B.E.F. was safely convoyed to France before the Germans had even learned of its departure.

(*b*) Admiral Beatty won a small victory in the Heligoland Bight ; this confirmed the Germans in their decision to remain on the defensive.

(*c*) Three British cruisers were sunk by the submarine U9 off Holland ; this was the first indication of the prominent *rôle* that under-water craft were later to play in the struggle for control of the sea.

(*d*) Scarborough, Hartlepool, and Yarmouth were bombarded by German cruisers.

(*e*) Early in 1915, cruisers on a similar raid were caught and roughly handled by Beatty in the Battle of the Dogger Bank ; after this coastal raids were abandoned. The strength of the British navy prevented any attempt being made to land German troops on British shores.

THE SWEEPING OF THE SEAS

The German cruisers abroad in August, 1914, sank little more than one per cent. of the British mercantile marine, but they were alarmingly active for some weeks.

(*a*) *The Karlsruhe* sank seventeen ships in a brief career off the West Indies.

(*b*) *The Kaiser Wilhelm der Grosse* made five captures before being sunk off West Africa.

(*c*) *The Konigsberg*, operating near Zanzibar, sank a battleship before being blocked in the Rufiji river ; its guns were later used in the defence of German East Africa.

(*d*) *The Pacific squadron*, under Admiral von Spee, was the only powerful flotilla. Leaving eastern waters before Japan declared war, and re-coaling at the Pacific Islands where news of the outbreak of war had not arrived, it steamed for the Chilean coast. Here it destroyed Admiral Craddock's squadron at the Battle of Coronel. Speed and secrecy in dispatching the *Invincible* and the *Inflexible* under Admiral Sturdee led to the destruction of Spee's flotilla at the Battle of the Falkland Islands.

(*e*) *The Emden* was the most destructive of the German raiders. It was detached from the Pacific fleet for service in the Indian Ocean. For three months it eluded every effort to locate it, but on November 9 its career was terminated by the Australian cruiser, *Sydney*. Details of the *Emden*'s adventures are shown in a separate map on p. 32.

GERMAN POSSESSIONS OVERSEAS CAPTURED

The need for re-coaling and refitting set a limit to the activities of all the German raiders, and the attack on German colonies was hastened in order to cut off their bases of supplies.

In the first month of the War a New Zealand contingent occupied Samoa, and in September Australia took control of German New Guinea. Tsingtao and Kiao-Chow,

MAP 10

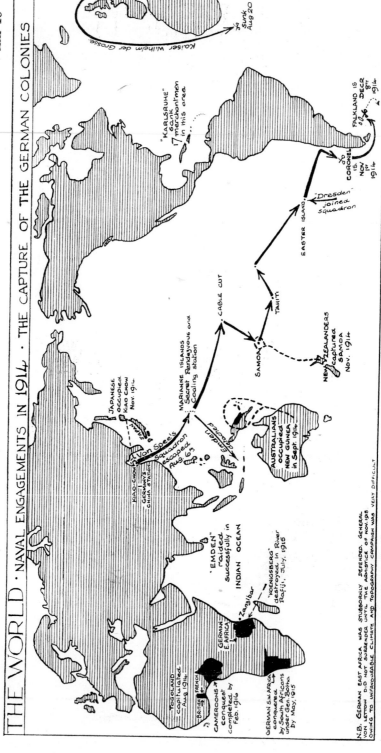

the German concession in Shantung, fell to the Japanese, who had entered the War in accordance with the Anglo-Japanese treaty of 1902.

In West Africa French and British forces attacked Togoland from both sides and, in a campaign which was brought to a close only in 1916, subjugated the Cameroons. In South Africa Britain had to contend with a rebellion, but it was put down without difficulty by Botha, the ex-Boer leader. South Africa rallied to the Empire at his words, " Now more than ever it is for the people of South Africa to practise the wise policy of forgive and forget." German South-west Africa was conquered by a force under Botha's command.

German East Africa, now known as Tanganyika, was attacked by Belgians, British, and Portuguese. The difficult nature of the country, however, skilfully exploited by the German generals, delayed its conquest until 1917, and a small force under General Lettow did not surrender until after the armistice of November, 1918.

South-eastern Europe (1914)

Although the War broke out in South-eastern Europe, this area played a rather negative *rôle* in 1914.

Austria failed to punish the Serbs for the Sarajevo murders. The Austrian army occupied Belgrade, but in less than a fortnight it was recaptured by the Serbs.

Italy failed to adhere to the Triple Alliance. In 1914 she declared her neutrality, and in 1915 she entered the War against her former allies. (See pp. 14 and 94.)

The Allied Fleets failed to intercept the German cruisers, *Goeben* and *Breslau*. Despite the overwhelming superiority of the Allied squadrons, these German ships succeeded in reaching Constantinople. Their arrival in Turkish waters was an event of supreme importance.

The Importance of the " Goeben " and " Breslau "

While it is possible that Turkey would have supported Germany in any case, the arrival of the *Goeben* and the *Breslau* made it certain, for German prestige and the influence of the pro-German Turks were notably enhanced by the event. Many Turks, including the Grand Vizier, were willing to fight Russia but loath to oppose the naval power of Great Britain. Their misgivings were now overcome, and Turkey joined the Central Powers. This had serious results for the Allies :

(*a*) The closing of the Straits subjected Russia to a blockade which seriously reduced her fighting-powers. Russia had greater reserves of man-power than any other combatant, but as a predominantly agricultural country she was dependent upon imports to equip and arm them. Access to foreign supplies, however, was difficult ; the White Sea ports were ice-bound for the greater part of the year, the Trans-Siberian railway was at this date still a single track, and the German fleet controlled the Baltic. Thus the closing of the Black Sea completed the isolation of Russia and was responsible for the pitiful state in which the Russian peasant armies had to face the German big guns.

(*b*) Turkish attacks on the Suez Canal and in the Caucasus, although repulsed, tied up large numbers of British and Russian troops in these remote theatres.

31

MAP II

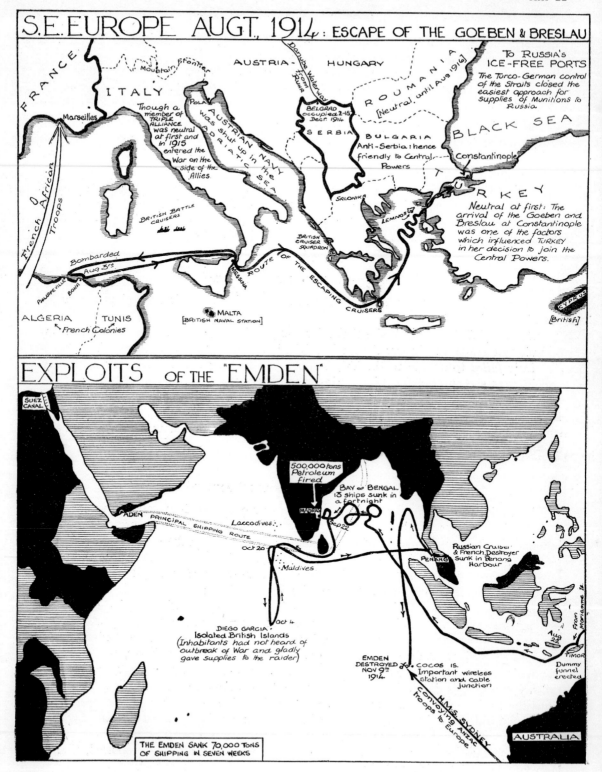

(*c*) The Gallipoli campaign followed and brought Great Britain heavy losses in lives and prestige.

THE WESTERN FRONT AFTER THE MARNE

I. THE 'RACE TO THE SEA'

When the German retreat in Champagne halted at the line of the Aisne, the battleground shifted to the north-west.

Each side extended its line northward in a series of unsuccessful attempts to outflank the other. These movements came to an end only when both lines reached the coast; after this there were no flanks to be turned.

II. THE GERMAN BID FOR THE STRAITS OF DOVER

Meanwhile the German forces released by the fall of Antwerp on October 10 tried to sweep down the coast and occupy the Channel ports. Had they succeeded, the coasts of Britain would have been threatened. Their advance was stemmed, however, by the Belgian army on the River Yser and by the B.E.F. at Ypres. On the Yser the flooding of the polders and at Ypres the sacrifice of over 50,000 men were necessary before the danger was averted.

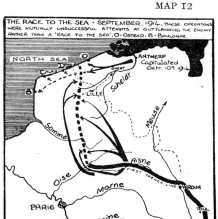

MAP 12

III. THE YSER

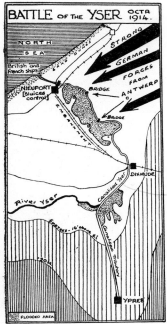

MAP 13

After their escape from Antwerp the Belgian troops took up a coastal position on the River Yser. Wisely refusing to join an Allied plan to advance inland, they succeeded in holding up the German army which threatened to occupy the Channel ports and the land behind the Allies. Attacking in force, the Germans crossed the river and threatened the railway embankment behind it, whereupon Belgian engineers manipulated the sea-locks at Nieuport. Thereupon the Germans were forced to retire to avoid being cut off by the water which slowly flooded the flat coastal plain.

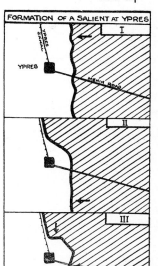

MAP 14

MAP 15

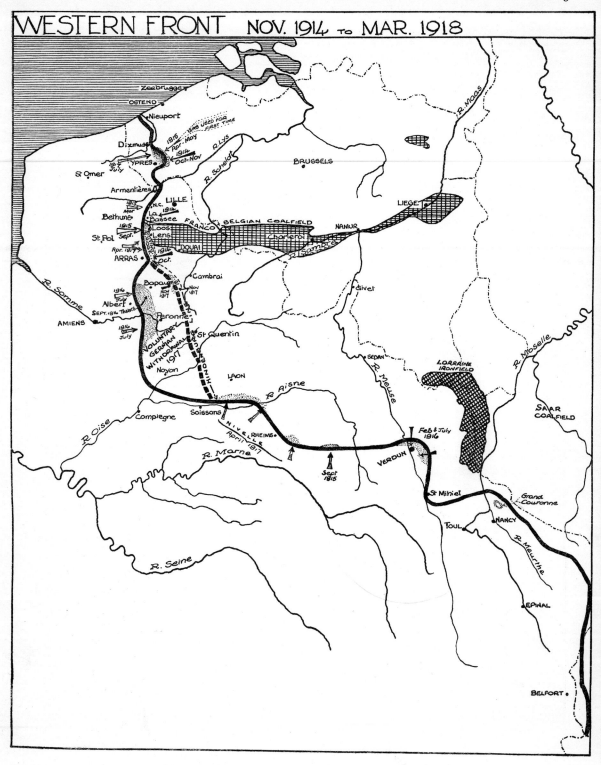

WESTERN FRONT NOV. 1914 to MAR. 1918

IV. THE FIRST BATTLE OF YPRES (1914)

South of the Yser line the Allied generals optimistically ordered an advance, but the Germans attacked in such force that the Allied troops could not even hold their own. The high land east of Ypres was held with difficulty, but the British troops were driven back on the north and the south. Thus was created the Ypres salient which was next subjected to converging attacks on either side. Twice the line was broken, but gallant counter-attacks prevented the Germans from breaking right through. When the battle came to an end the greater part of the salient remained in Allied hands. It was dearly bought and thereafter constituted a death-trap for its defenders, for it was commanded on three sides by German artillery.

STALEMATE

When the Battle of Ypres petered out, the Germans had failed in their second great effort to win the War in the west. A new phase in the War now started ; the lines extended unbroken from the North Sea to Switzerland, and they became almost stationary. Methods of war hitherto unknown developed ; battles, instead of bringing victory or defeat at the end of the day, went on for months and still failed to bring about a decision. Machine-guns and elaborate trenches soon placed any attacking force at a serious disadvantage, and so for over two years no vital defeat was suffered by either side, for neither possessed the key to successful attack.

How could the deadlock in the west be broken ? Many alternative solutions were proposed.

I. THE WESTERNERS

The generals in command on the western front thought that the key to the problem was to get more and more men, and so to mass them against a small sector of the enemy's line that they would break through, cause a general retreat, and possibly end the War. At the expense of millions of casualties this was tried time after time and never succeeded. These massed attacks were supported by preliminary artillery bombardment intended to break up the wire entanglements and to drive the defenders from their machine-guns. In 1915, however, the shells were too few and too poor in quality to do this. The British generals in France maintained their faith in the importance of their own theatre of war and steadfastly opposed ' side-shows ' like the Dardanelles. The majority of the French took the same view, because the Germans occupied the sacred soil of France with four-fifths of its coal and most of its iron-ore. Strangely enough, the generals also obstructed the introduction of new instruments of war which were rapidly being evolved.

II. NEW INSTRUMENTS OF WAR

Under this heading should be noted :

(a) Kitchener's Army

Forecasting a three-year war, Kitchener appealed for volunteers for a new army, and nearly a million men responded before the end of 1914. For the first time Britain created a national army of continental dimensions.

MAP 16

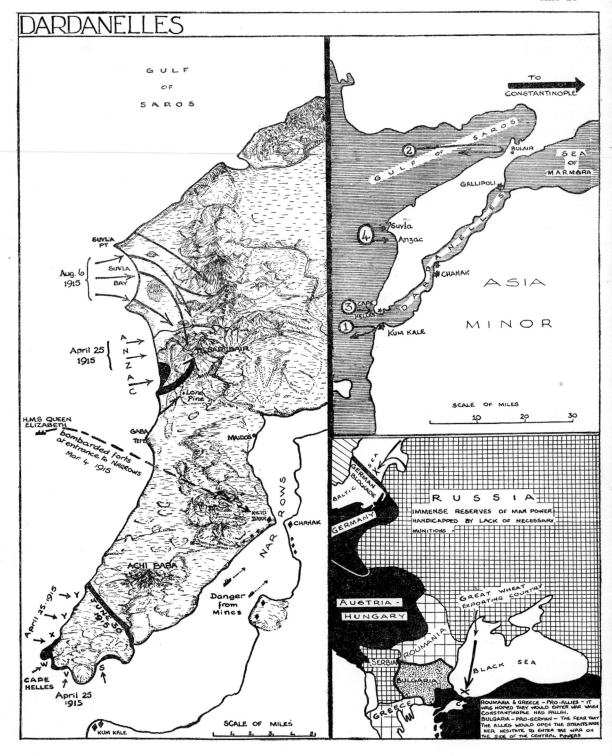

DARDANELLES

GULF

OF

SAROS

SUVLA
PT

Aug. 6
1915

SUVLA
BAY

ERT
LAKE

April 25
1915

A
N
Z
A
C

•Lone
Pine

H.M.S QUEEN
ELIZABETH

bombarded forts
at entrance to NARROWS
Mar. 4 1915

GABA
TEPE

MAIDOS

ACHI BABA

April 25 1915
Y
Y

April 25 1915
X

TURKS 30 1915

X

CAPE
HELLES
April 25
1915

V
S

N
A
R
R
O
W
S

KILID
BAHR

CHANAK

Danger
from
Mines

SCALE OF MILES
1   2   3   4   5

KUM KALE

TO
CONSTANTINOPLE

GULF OF SAROS

② BULAIR

GALLIPOLI

SEA
OF
MARMORA

④ Suvla
Anzac

③ CAPE
HELLES

① CHANAK

KUM KALE

ASIA

MINOR

SCALE OF MILES
10   20   30

SEA

BALTIC

GERMAN
BLOCKADE

GERMANY

RUSSIA

IMMENSE RESERVES OF MAN POWER
HANDICAPPED BY LACK OF NECESSARY
MUNITIONS

AUSTRIA-
HUNGARY

GREAT WHEAT
EXPORTING COUNTRY

SERBIA

ROUMANIA

BLACK SEA

BULGARIA

GREECE

ROUMANIA & GREECE - PRO-ALLIES - IT
WAS HOPED THEY WOULD ENTER WAR WHEN
CONSTANTINOPLE HAD FALLEN.
BULGARIA - PRO-GERMAN - THE FEAR THAT
THE ALLIES WOULD OPEN THE STRAITS MADE
HER HESITATE TO ENTER THE WAR ON
THE SIDE OF THE CENTRAL POWERS

(b) Provision of New Types of Guns and Shells

Shrapnel, although murderous against troops in the open, proved ineffective in trench warfare, and the *Stokes* gun or trench-mortar was introduced to project missiles up and into the opposing trenches. Complaints of a shortage of high explosives to demolish the German fortifications led to an English newspaper campaign and to the formation of a Coalition Government.

(c) A Ministry of Munitions

This was formed under Lloyd George, who speeded up the production of all kinds of war-materials and greatly increased the supply of machine-guns, invaluable in defence.

(d) The Tank

The two chief obstacles to offensive measures were machine-guns and trench-fortifications. As early as October, 1914, Colonel Swinton proposed the tank—a car armoured against machine-gun fire and provided with caterpillar traction to surmount the trench-barriers. Soldiers, however, dismissed the device as a 'toy,' and it was not employed until 1916.

(e) The Use of Gas at the Second Battle of Ypres

Germany, too, was busy preparing surprises, and on April 22, 1915, the Allied troops on the western front first faced a gas-attack. Warnings that its use was impending had been ignored, and the Germans achieved a complete surprise. They broke through the northern half of the Ypres salient, making a gap over four miles in width. The Allies were saved from overwhelming disaster by the German failure to provide adequate reserves.

(f) The 'Easterners'

Many thoughtful strategists contended that if the German lines in France were impregnable the proper course would be to concentrate attack upon the weaker Central Powers, *i.e.*, Turkey and Austria. Thus originated the campaigns in Gallipoli and Salonika.

THE DARDANELLES (1915)

The immediate cause of the attempt to force the Dardanelles was a Russian request for a diversion against the Turks, who had advanced in the Caucasus. The campaign, however, had much wider possibilities ; it offered a way out of the deadlock in France, it promised to break the virtual blockade of Russia, and it might persuade hesitant Balkan countries to embrace the Allied cause.

General French pressed the claims of the western front to all the available troops, and so the first attack on the Dardanelles was undertaken on February 19 by the Navy alone. During the three months which had elapsed since Turkey entered the War, the fortresses at the entrance to the Straits had been restored and the British fleet made slow progress. The grand attack was not made until March 19, and in it three Allied ships struck mines and sank. Despite orders to persevere, the local commander took the mistaken view that further progress was impossible without military aid. A further month elapsed, and the Turks were well prepared when the troops were landed on April 25.

THE GALLIPOLI LANDINGS

The military attack was well planned by Ian Hamilton, the Allied commander. The Turks were kept in ignorance of the intended landing-places by well-conceived bluffs : (1) the French made a temporary landing on the Asiatic side ; (2) a naval division staged a mock landing at Bulair, where the Turks expected the attack and where they massed all their reserves ; (3) the main attack was made at Cape Helles ; (4) a flank-attack was made by the Australian and New Zealand Army Corps (A.N.Z.A.C.) north of Gaba Tepe.

The main landings were made on five beaches, S, V, W, X, and Y, and were mismanaged. At S and X beaches the troops, although feebly opposed, made no advance inland. W and V beaches, on either side of Cape Helles, proved death-traps ; as the troops landed they were swept by deadly machine-gun fire from concealed Turkish posts in the heights above. Y beach was occupied without opposition, and its troops might have taken the Cape Helles defenders in the rear and played a decisive part in the main attack. Instead, however, they were ignominiously re-embarked following a Turkish counter-attack in the night. The Anzac troops landed with ease but failed to secure the important heights on account of the difficulty of the ground, the weight of their packs, and the counter-attacks of Mustapha Kemal (later Dictator of post-War Turkey).

The failure of the initial attacks really meant the failure of the campaign, for the Turks brought up reinforcements which, aided by German generalship and the natural advantages of the high ground, not only sufficed to hold up the innumerable attacks subsequently made, but also took a cruel toll of the attackers.

The troops in Gallipoli suffered terrific losses ; they had no base where they might snatch some respite from being continually under fire, and they endured bad water, disease, flies, and, later, frost-bite. On August 6, reinforcements having arrived, a new landing was made at Suvla Bay. Here, too, the invaders failed to secure the high land and became another target for Turkish snipers. Finally, at the end of 1915, it was decided to withdraw, and the withdrawal was accomplished without loss on December 18 and January 8. Thus ended an unhappy campaign ; its original conception was excellent, its execution imperfect, and its conclusion admirable.

THE EASTERN AND SOUTH–EASTERN FRONTS (1915)

Early in 1915 Falkenhayn, who had succeeded Moltke as the German Chief of Staff, planned to destroy Serbia and to open up a free line of communications with Turkey. The necessary assistance of Bulgaria was assured, for the Bulgars still smarted from the loss of Macedonia in 1913, but the attack on Serbia was not launched until October.

Earlier in the year the Russians had occupied Przemysl and several Carpathian passes which threatened the Hungarian plain. The Balkan campaign had, therefore, to wait until the Russians had been pressed back to a safe distance.

THE GREAT WAR (1914–1918)

I. RUSSIAN RETREAT (1915)

(1) In April, therefore, the Austrian army in Galicia was stiffened by German troops and placed under the leadership of Mackensen, who was possibly the most brilliant of the German generals in the War. An over-whelming artillery bombardment shattered the Russian defences, and Mackensen broke right through their lines at Gorlice and subsequently reoccupied practically all Galicia.

(2a and 2b) During the summer a pincer-like movement from north and south enforced the evacuation of Warsaw and the loss of 750,000 prisoners together with the whole of Poland.

(3) In the autumn new attacks led the Russians to withdraw to a straighter line more than 200 miles east of Warsaw.

After this defeat Russia never seriously threatened Germany, but she compelled the Central Powers to keep troops in the east when they were urgently needed in the west.

MAP 17

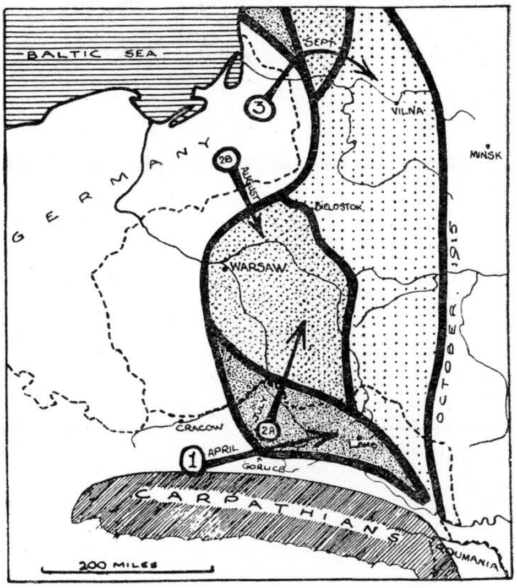

EASTERN FRONT:
THE RUSSIAN RETREAT (1915)

II. THE ITALIAN FRONT

Meanwhile Italy had declared war on Austria, but the mountain barrier of the Alps enabled the Central Powers to withstand attack on the River Isonzo, where trench-warfare set in.

III. OCCUPATION OF SERBIA

The threatened attack on Serbia started on October 6, when the Austrians advanced across the Danube in force. A week later the Bulgars attacked the Serbs in the flank and rear. The Serbian army was cut off from Salonika, where Allied troops had been landed to help them ; the Serbs were forced to retreat through the mountains of Albania, where they suffered severely from the rigours of the winter and at the hands of bandits. The survivors reaching the Adriatic were rescued by Allied ships and later sent to join the Salonika army. The Central Powers now controlled a large area extending from the North Sea to Arabia.

IV. SALONIKA

The troops landed here by France and Britain were intended to enable Greece to support the Serbs. They arrived too few and too late to fulfil this purpose. Venizelos, the Greek Prime Minister, who had arranged the landing with the Allies, was immediately dismissed by King Constantine. The Allied forces did little of military value until 1918, when their numbers had risen to 500,000.

V. MESOPOTAMIA

British forces had occupied Basra in 1914 in order to control the oil-wells north

MAP 18

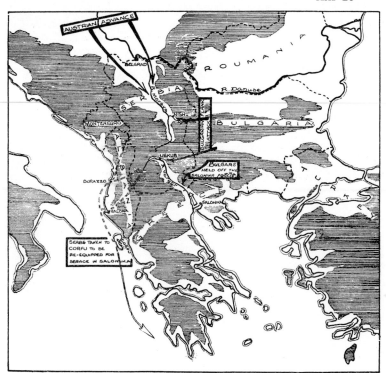

THE BALKANS: COLLAPSE OF SERBIA

MAP 19

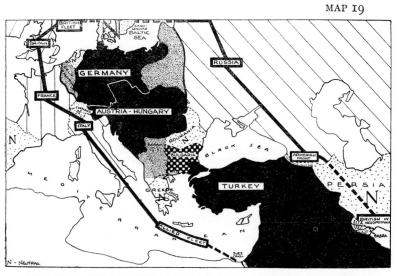

EUROPE: THE CENTRALITY OF THE GERMAN ALLIANCE

of the Persian Gulf. In 1915 General Townshend was sent forward up the valley, and his spectacular successes at Amara and Kut, at a time when success was rare, led to further unwarrantable advance. He was besieged by the Turks at Kut and forced to surrender in April, 1916.

1916

During 1916 both sides concentrated their efforts on the western front, although the Allies made some efforts to synchronize offensives on all the fronts.

I. VERDUN

From February to December there was heavy fighting before the famous French fortress of Verdun. Falkenhayn decided to attack at this point because he knew the French would make any sacrifice to retain possession of so famous a stronghold. His idea was not to break through, but to draw all the French reserves into the line to be blasted by the heavy artillery he concentrated in the Verdun sector. As he had anticipated, the French losses were exceedingly heavy, and the morale of their troops suffered, but the cost in German lives made it doubtful whether this policy of attrition was a wise one. The French retained Verdun partly through the stubbornness of their defence and partly through the opening of the Battle of the Somme, which drew German troops away to another part of the line.

II. THE BATTLE OF THE SOMME

Great Britain was now ready to take a larger share in the military operations in France. By the middle of 1916, thanks to Kitchener's army of civilian volunteers, the number of British troops in France had risen from 90,000 to a million, despite 500,000 casualties and 500,000 engaged in distant theatres of war. Moreover, the British Parliament had now authorized conscription, so that an even larger number of men could be drawn upon.

It was hoped that the weight of numbers would break the German lines, and this was the aim of the Battle of the Somme. Douglas Haig, who had succeeded Sir John French as commander of the Expeditionary Force, made prolonged preparations for the battle. He sacrificed all hopes of surprising the enemy by a preliminary bombardment lasting a week. Even so, the German defences were undestroyed, and the infantry attack on July 1 cost 60,000 casualties without achieving the expected break-through. Such losses were unprecedented in history, but the spirits of the troops were unbroken. The battle, in which the French and British attacked side by side, continued until November, and at a cost of 600,000 casualties the Allies advanced thirty miles. Much of the territory gained, however, had no strategic value,

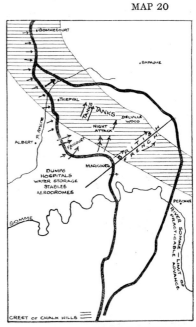

MAP 20

THE BATTLE OF THE SOMME (1916)

41

MAP 21

ITALIAN FRONT

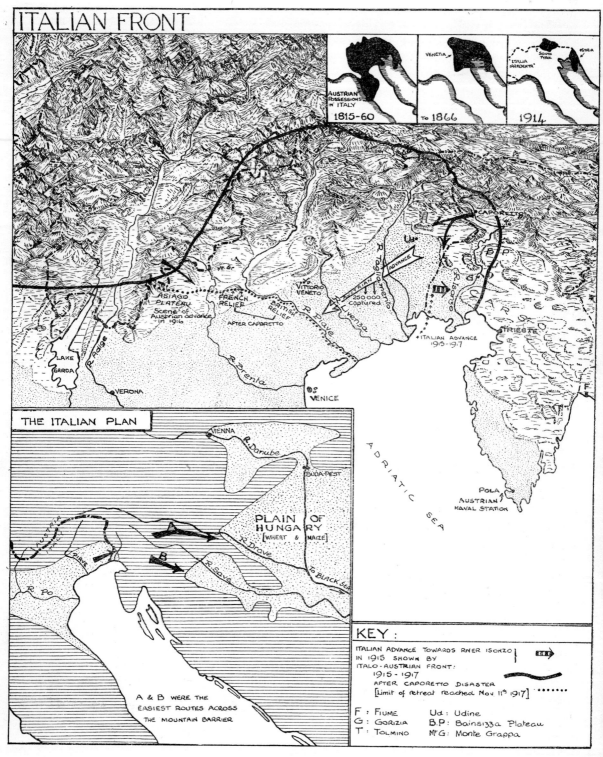

AUSTRIAN POSSESSIONS IN ITALY 1815-60

VENETIA · to 1866

ITALIA IRREDENTA · SOUTH TYROL · ISTRIA · 1914

ASIAGO PLATEAU
Scene of Austrian advance in 1916

Mte. Gr.

FRENCH RELIEF

BRITISH RELIEF
AFTER CAPORETTO

VITTORIO VENETO

250,000 Captured

R. Tagliamento

Ud.

ITALIAN ADVANCE

CAPORETTO

B.P

R. Isonzo

TRIESTE

CARSO

+ITALIAN ADVANCE 1915-1917

R. Adige

R. Piave

R. Livenza

R. Brenta

LAKE GARDA

VERONA

VENICE

ADRIATIC SEA

POLA
AUSTRIAN NAVAL STATION

THE ITALIAN PLAN

VIENNA
R. Danube
BUDA-PEST

PLAIN OF HUNGARY
[WHEAT & MAIZE]

R. Drave
R. Save
To BLACK SEA

AUSTRIA TYROL

PIAVE

R. PO

A & B WERE THE EASIEST ROUTES ACROSS THE MOUNTAIN BARRIER

KEY:

ITALIAN ADVANCE TOWARDS RIVER ISONZO IN 1915 SHOWN BY
ITALO-AUSTRIAN FRONT:
1915 - 1917
AFTER CAPORETTO DISASTER
[Limit of retreat reached Nov 11th 1917]

F : Fiume   Ud : Udine
G : Gorizia   B.P : Bainsizza Plateau
T : Tolmino   MtG : Monte Grappa

and at the end of the year the French army was definitely war-weary. The German losses were not so heavy, but they increased in the later stages and caused a deterioration in the morale of the German troops.

The battle was notable for the valuable assistance rendered by aircraft in reconnaissance-work and for the first use of tanks which later proved the most successful innovation of the War.

III. THE ITALIAN FRONT

The Chantilly Conference in December, 1915, had arranged for an Italian offensive against the Plain of Hungary to take place at the same time as the Battle of the Somme. The Austrians attacked first, however, and the Italians had to ward off a dangerous threat from the Trentino. The Italian offensive, therefore, did not start till the autumn and then made little progress.

IV. THE EASTERN FRONT

Despite their cruel defeats in 1915, the Russians took the offensive in March, 1916, near Lake Narocz as a diversion on behalf of Verdun. On June 4, in response to Italian appeals, Brussilov launched another attack in Galicia. Brussilov was a brilliant general and scored a great success ; he captured 350,000 men, he relieved the pressure in the west and in Italy, and his advance in Galicia induced Roumania to embrace the Allied cause. The cost paid was the loss of a million Russian troops. This was Russia's last effort ; time after time her troops had sacrificed themselves for the Allies, and by this time they were utterly exhausted.

V. ROUMANIA

Encouraged by the Russian advance, Roumania, long sympathetic to the Allies, entered the War. Her troops optimistically invaded Hungary, but a German-Bulgarian army entering the Dubrudja took them in the rear, and a German-Austrian army threw them back over the Carpathians. Caught between two fires, the Roumanians had to abandon the capital, Bucharest, and the greater part of their country. Their invaluable supplies of wheat and oil fell into the hands of the Central Powers.

THE WAR AT SEA AFTER 1914

During the War many English people were disappointed that no great sea-battle was won by the British fleet ; they did not realize the tremendous importance of the naval blockade which slowly starved the Germans of essential war-materials. As early as July, 1914, the British fleet established control over the commercial shipping of the North Sea, and in March, 1915, Germany replied by declaring that the approaches to the British Isles constituted a war-zone where she would seek to destroy every hostile merchant ship. Thus began the first ' submarine campaign,' in which allied and neutral ships were sunk without warning. Neutral powers had resented the British search-parties which boarded their ships, but they were outraged by the German methods and the loss of life resulting. The indignation of the U.S.A reached a climax in May, 1915, when the *Lusitania* was sunk and over a thousand passengers were drowned. In deference to American protests—renewed in 1916—the Germans abandoned these indiscriminate attacks.

The German Admiral, Scheer, now determined to hazard a fleet-engagement. Nothing had happened to offset the British naval superiority, but the pressure of the blockade made it necessary to take some risks. He planned to destroy Beatty's cruiser-squadron by engaging it with the whole of the German High Seas Fleet.

I. THE BATTLE OF JUTLAND (MAY 31, 1916)

The battle which resulted took place off Jutland. The course of the engagement was very confused, but the following points are clear :

(*a*) The British fleet was prepared; the Grand Fleet was ordered to sea, and the German attempt to isolate and destroy part of it was frustrated.

(*b*) British caution and the fear of a submarine ambush permitted the German fleet to make good its escape when it might have been cut off and destroyed.

(*c*) German tactics, ship-construction, and gunnery proved in many ways superior to those of the British, who suffered much the more serious losses.

(*d*) The German fleet was once more driven off the seas.

(*e*) Most important of all, the battle gave the Germans no alternative but to renew and intensify their submarine campaign. This had momentous results in 1917.

II. UNRESTRICTED SUBMARINE WARFARE (1917)

On February 1, 1917, the German naval authorities embarked on a campaign of indiscriminate submarine warfare. The support of the military leaders enabled them to overcome the scruples of the politicians who feared the political consequences of this ruthless measure. The under-water fleet was greatly augmented and received orders to sink at sight any vessel in British water. Thus it was hoped to bring Britain to her knees in six months.

The amount of damage which could be done when submarines were allowed to sink ships without warning had not been exaggerated. In the month of April alone over a million tons of shipping was sent to the bottom; one ship out of four leaving British shores never reached port. Jellicoe himself admitted that the Germans would win the War "unless we can stop these losses." When asked if there were no solution to the problem, he replied, "Absolutely none that we can see now." A remedy was found through the initiative of Lloyd George, who had succeeded Asquith as Prime Minister in December, 1916, and by the end of 1917 the peril was past.

The most important defensive measure was the adoption of the 'Convoy System.' The capital ships of the fleet had always been protected by an escort of destroyers. Now merchant ships, too, were assembled in fleets to sail under similar naval protection. This procedure was very successful, and 99½ per cent. of the convoyed ships arrived safely. In addition, active measures were taken to attack the submarines by mines and depth-charges. Aeroplanes and hydrophones were employed to detect the presence of the under-water craft, which began to suffer severely. The effects of the campaign were also counteracted by increased ship-building and by increased agricultural production in Britain. In 1918 the Dover patrol attacked the submarine bases of Zeebrugge and Ostend and blocked their exits. This did not completely prevent submarines from leaving harbour, but the enterprise took place at a time of serious military reverses and did much to restore British optimism. The assistance of the United States' fleet and the determination of the British people—particularly the seamen who refused to be scared off the sea—were equally important factors in defeating this desperate German campaign.

THE HOME FRONT

Essentially the aim of war is to destroy the enemy's will to resist ; the destruction of her armies is only a means to this end. In the Great War additional means were employed which brought the War home to the civilian populations as never before.

From the beginning encroachments were made on civil liberties. In Britain the Defence of the Realm Act (' Dora ') gave rise to a host of police regulations and restrictions. Suspected spies were imprisoned without trial, food-hoarding became a punishable offence, and people were fined for failing to draw the blinds at night.

Taxation became crushing, and all kinds of industries were converted for the output of war-materials. The manufacture of luxuries ceased, but even so, the essential industries were handicapped by a shortage of workers. In England alone over four million men were enlisted in the army, and women were extensively employed in their places.

Towards the end of the War the people on both sides suffered intensely from the shortage of food caused by the blockades. The death-rate of civilians in Germany was trebled in 1917. In every country the Government was compelled to control the distribution of foodstuffs. Butter and sugar were unobtainable, and in England people ate standard bread made from adulterated flour.

From January, 1915, onward London and neighbouring districts were subjected to German air-raids, first by Zeppelins and later by aeroplanes. Altogether 4000 casualties resulted, and the nervous strain severely tried the under-nourished population. Later, reprisals were undertaken against German towns.

Governments resorted to propaganda to maintain the spirits of their war-weary peoples. In England the Press stimulated a hysterical hatred of the Germans by publishing untrue tales of atrocities. Even official communiqués exaggerated successes and minimized reverses. The German people were similarly hoodwinked. Propaganda also sought to undermine the morale of the enemy. Germany subsidized seditious French newspapers, and Lord Northcliffe, controller of British propaganda, arranged for subversive pamphlets to come into the hands of German soldiers.

THE WESTERN FRONT (1917)

Public dissatisfaction with the conduct of the War had led to a change of Government in Britain and brought a change in the military command in France. Joffre was succeeded by Nivelle, who, like his predecessor, pinned his faith on a gigantic breakthrough. His April offensive in Champagne was prefaced by a British attack near Arras in which the Canadian troops captured Vimy Ridge. Nivelle's own offensive was a shocking failure. It had been preceded by a voluntary German retirement to a strongly fortified position called the ' Hindenburg line.' This German move ruined the whole basis of Nivelle's scheme. Nevertheless, he persevered blindly and was so

MAP 22

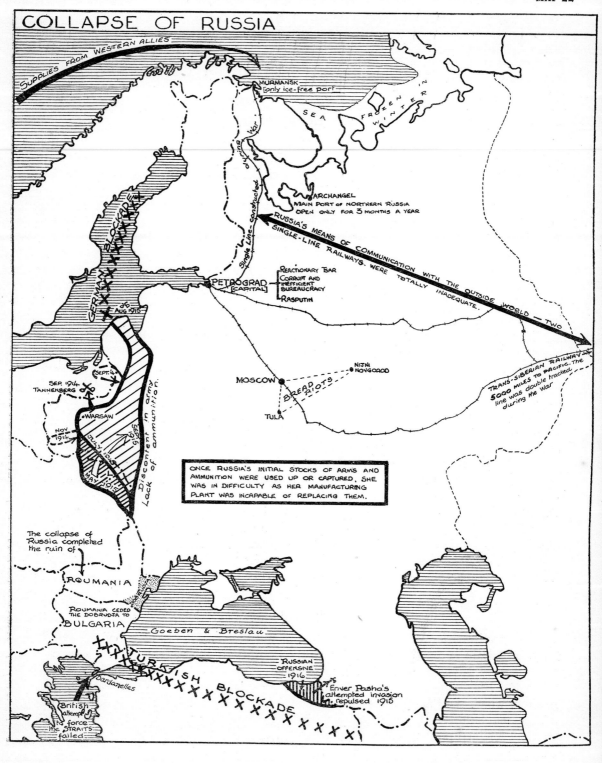

COLLAPSE OF RUSSIA

SUPPLIES FROM WESTERN ALLIES

MURMANSK
[only ice-free port]

SEA FROZEN IN WINTER

GERMAN BLOCKADE

Single line constructed during War

ARCHANGEL
MAIN PORT OF NORTHERN RUSSIA
OPEN ONLY FOR 3 MONTHS A YEAR

RUSSIA'S MEANS OF COMMUNICATION WITH THE OUTSIDE WORLD — TWO SINGLE-LINE RAILWAYS WERE TOTALLY INADEQUATE.

Single Line constructed

× Aug. 1915

PETROGRAD
[CAPITAL]

REACTIONARY TSAR
CORRUPT AND
INEFFICIENT
BUREAUCRACY
RASPUTIN

SEPT. 14.

SEP. 1914.
TANNENBERG

NOV
1914.

Warsaw

Discontent in army. Lack of ammunition.

MAY 1915

MOSCOW

NIJNI
NOVGOROD

BREAD RIOTS

TULA

TRANS-SIBERIAN RAILWAY
5000 MILES TO PACIFIC. The line was double tracked during the War

ONCE RUSSIA'S INITIAL STOCKS OF ARMS AND
AMMUNITION WERE USED UP OR CAPTURED, SHE
WAS IN DIFFICULTY AS HER MANUFACTURING
PLANT WAS INCAPABLE OF REPLACING THEM.

The collapse of
Russia completed
the ruin of

ROUMANIA

ROUMANIA CEDED
THE DOBRUDJA TO
BULGARIA

Goeben & Breslau

RUSSIAN
OFFENSIVE
1916

TURKISH BLOCKADE

Dardanelles

Enver Pasha's
attempted invasion
repulsed 1915

British
attempt
to force
the STRAITS
failed

severely defeated that the French armies mutinied, refusing any longer to engage in futile and suicidal offensives. Nivelle was replaced by Pétain, a sound general who succeeded in restoring discipline and some measure of confidence by standing on the defensive to await the American reinforcements. In order to relieve the French during this period of weakness, and hoping to win the War by a solo British effort, Haig now undertook the third Battle of Ypres.

The battle started with General Plumer's carefully prepared and highly successful seizure of Messines Ridge, from which the Germans had overlooked the Ypres salient. The main offensive was not so well conceived. The troops were sent to the attack across the clay plain, which a preliminary bombardment of 4,250,000 shells had transformed into a sea of mud. Moreover, the Germans had the advantage of the higher land, and the British troops suffered 300,000 losses. The offensive continued from July until November and culminated in the bloody attack on Passchendaele, which finally convinced Haig and the whole world that his tactics were faulty.

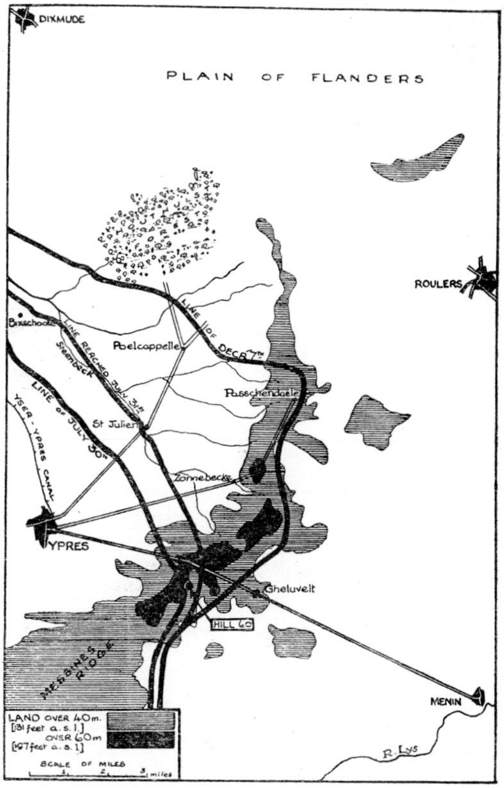

MAP 23

WESTERN FRONT (1917)

New Allies for Old

In 1915 Serbia had been destroyed, and in 1916, Roumania. In 1917 the French were reduced to impotence by the May mutinies, the Italians were thrown into disorder by the defeat at Caporetto, and the Russian Revolution caused a complete breakdown on the Eastern front.

I. THE CAPORETTO DÉBÂCLE

From 1915 onward the Italians had made eleven offensives on the Isonzo front without tangible success. The Austrian defences, however, were cracking, and in October, 1917, Germany sent reinforcements to enable her ally to take the offensive. Aided by the war-weariness of the Italians and their faulty defence, the Central Powers gained a great victory at Caporetto. The Italian retreat became a rout. French and British assistance had to be sent to Italy, but the Italian troops recovered their confidence and re-established their line on the River Piave before their Allies were actually engaged.

II. THE COLLAPSE OF RUSSIA

After two and a half years of loyal service to the Allied cause, Russia completely collapsed. In March, 1917, revolution and the abdication of the Czar were followed by

MAP 24

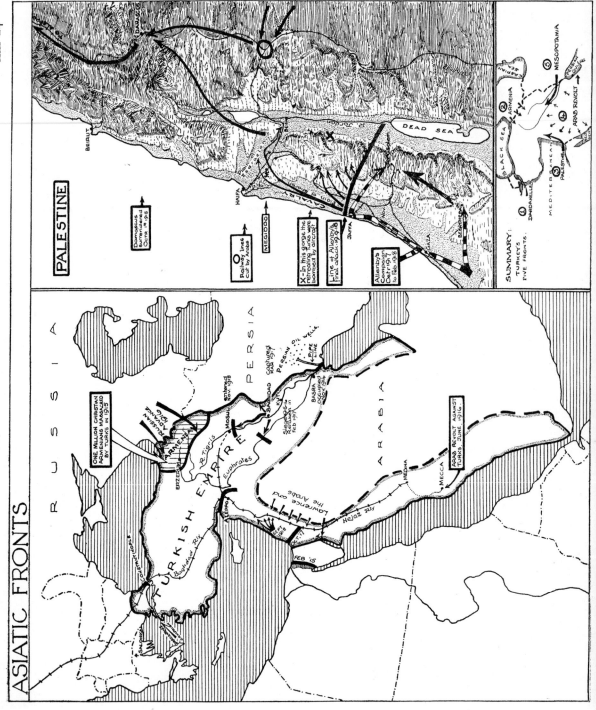

ASIATIC FRONTS

PALESTINE

Damascus surrendered Oct. 1st. 1918

MEGIDDO

Railway lines cut by Arabs

X - in this gorge the retreating Turks were bombed by aircraft

Line of Allenby's final attack 19.9.18

Allenby's Campaign Oct. 1917 to Feb. 1918

BEIRUT

HAIFA

DEAD SEA

JAFFA

GAZA

SUMMARY:
TURKEY'S
FIVE FRONTS.

① DARDANELLES
② ARMENIA
③ PALESTINE
④ ARAB REVOLT
⑤ MESOPOTAMIA

BLACK SEA
CASPIAN SEA
MEDITERRANEAN

RUSSIA

PERSIA

TURKISH EMPIRE

ARABIA

ONE MILLION CHRISTIAN ARMENIANS MASSACRED BY TURKS IN 1915

RUSSIAN ADVANCE 1916

ARMENIA

ERZERUM

MOSUL

Entered Nov. 1918

BAGDAD

Captured MAR 1917

PERSIAN OIL WELLS

PIPE LINE

KUT

Siege broken in Feb 1917

BASRA Occupied 1914

R. Tigris

Euphrates

ALEPPO

Lawrence and the Arabs

Hejaz Rly

MEDINA

MECCA

ARAB REVOLT AGAINST TURKS. JUNE. 1916.

FEB. '15

Bagdad Rly

CONSTANTINOPLE

SALONIKA

Baghdad Rly

wholesale desertions from the army. A provisional Government attempted to continue the War, but its depleted and demoralized army gave way before a German offensive against Riga. In November the Bolsheviks seized power, and in December they concluded an armistice with the Central Powers. Many German troops had already been freed for the western front by Russia's weakness, and by March, 1918, thirty-two divisions had been transferred thither from the east.

For the history of the revolution, see pp. 55–57.

III. THE U.S.A. AND THE WAR

America broke off diplomatic relations with Germany immediately the submarine campaign was renewed and declared war on April 6, 1917. In reality the scale on which the States had provided the Allies with war-materials made her an ally from the first. Nevertheless, the U.S.A. had been so long determined to avoid military participation that they were ill prepared when war was declared and were unable to assist the campaign in France until 1918.

Psychologically, however, the American contribution was very great. The thought of the States' unlimited resources of men and materials sustained the Allies in the dark days when everything went wrong. Ultimate defeat became unthinkable, and America's entry into the War made the German task of destroying Britain's will to resist an impossible one.

Immediate practical help was forthcoming in April, 1917, in the provision of cruisers to assist the convoying of merchantmen, to attack submarines, and to tighten up the blockade of Germany. Financial support was also arranged, without which the Allies would have been hard pressed.

By the end of the War America had nearly two million men in France, and they not only succoured the Allies during the great 1918 retreat, but took over about 100 miles of front for the final assault on the German lines.

THE MIDDLE EAST

It was in the Middle East that the Central Powers first began to crack. In Mesopotamia and Egypt the British had taken the offensive quite early in the War, but until 1917 their advance had been slow and halting.

I. MESOPOTAMIA

After the fall of Kut (see p. 41) the forces here were reorganized by General Maude, who made a methodical advance and occupied Bagdad in March, 1917. Thereafter preparations were made for the permanent occupation of the country, and Mosul and its oil-field were not occupied until after the Turkish armistice of October, 1918.

II. PALESTINE

Having constructed a pipe-line to bring water from the Nile, the Egyptian forces crossed the desert and reached Gaza, the gateway to Palestine, in March, 1917. After an unsuccessful assault on the town, General Murray was superseded by Allenby, who broke through the Turkish line at Beersheba and occupied Jaffa and Jerusalem by the end of the year.

D

MAP 25

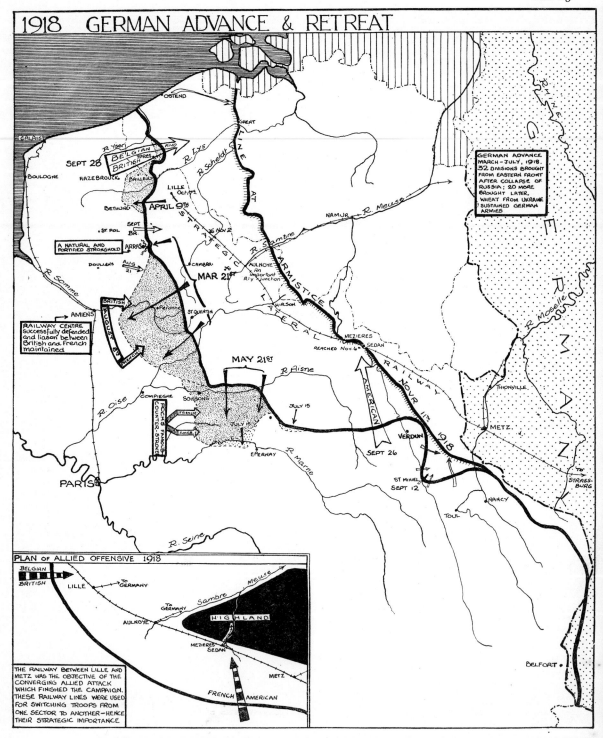

1918 GERMAN ADVANCE & RETREAT

OSTEND

GHENT

CALAIS

R. Yser

BELGIAN AND BRITISH

YPRES

SEPT 28

R. Lys

R. Scheldt

RHINE

BOULOGNE

HAZEBROUCK

BAILLEUL

BETHUNE

LILLE Oct 17th

APRIL 9TH

NAMUR

R. Meuse

A NATURAL AND FORTIFIED STRONGHOLD

ST POL

SEPT BR

ARRAS

Nov 2

R. Sambre

GERMAN ADVANCE MARCH – JULY, 1918. 32 DIVISIONS BROUGHT FROM EASTERN FRONT AFTER COLLAPSE OF RUSSIA; 20 MORE BROUGHT LATER. WHEAT FROM UKRAINE SUSTAINED GERMAN ARMIES

DOULLENS

AUG 21

CAMBRAI

MAR 21st

AULNOYE An important Rly Junction

R. Somme

BRITISH AUGUST 8th ATTACK

PERONNE

ST QUENTIN

RAILWAY CENTRE successfully defended and liaison between British and French maintained

AMIENS

HIRSON

R. Moselle

STRATEGIC

LATERAL

RAILWAY

ARMISTICE

MEZIERES

SEDAN

REACHED NOV 6th

TIHONVILLE

MAY 21ST

R. Aisne

AMERICAN

NOV 11th 1918

METZ

R. Oise

COMPIEGNE

SOISSONS

FRENCH

FOCH'S FAMOUS COUNTER-STROKE

AMER.

JULY 18th

JULY 15

VERDUN

SEPT 26

STRASS-BURG

EPERNAY

R. Marne

ST MIHIEL SEPT 12

PARIS

NANCY

TOUL

R. Seine

GERMANY

BELFORT

PLAN of ALLIED OFFENSIVE 1918

BELGIAN BRITISH

LILLE

To GERMANY

Meuse

To GERMANY

Sambre

HIGHLAND

AULNOYE

MEZIERES SEDAN

METZ

FRENCH AMERICAN

THE RAILWAY BETWEEN LILLE AND METZ WAS THE OBJECTIVE OF THE CONVERGING ALLIED ATTACK WHICH FINISHED THE CAMPAIGN. THESE RAILWAY LINES WERE USED FOR SWITCHING TROOPS FROM ONE SECTOR TO ANOTHER—HENCE THEIR STRATEGIC IMPORTANCE

In September, 1918, a final victory was achieved and the Turkish armies were completely destroyed at the Battle of Megiddo. The Turkish right wing was shattered, and while the cavalry rode through to cut off the line of retreat northward, the infantry wheeled eastward and drove the disorganized Turks through the hills to the River Jordan and the merciless Arabs beyond. At the same time as the Turkish armistice was being arranged in Europe, Damascus and Aleppo were also occupied.

III. COLONEL LAWRENCE AND THE ARAB REVOLT

Between the Palestine and the Mesopotamian fronts the Turks had to contend with an Arab revolt which broke out at Mecca in 1916. The Arabs' remarkable mobility in the desert was utilized and organized by T. E. Lawrence, a young British officer who attained an amazing ascendancy over the Arab people. Under his leadership the Arabs threatened Turkish communications by many raids on the Hejaz Railway and succeeded in drawing away large bodies of Turkish troops from the Palestine front. In September, 1918, they made a diversion east of Jordan which played an important part in Allenby's victory at Megiddo.

Lawrence sponsored the Arab claims to the conquered territory, but he failed to get their claims fully recognized at the Peace Conference because of a secret arrangement with France by which the territory had already been parcelled out.

THE GERMAN OFFENSIVES (1918)

For three years every attempt to decide the issue on the western front had proved a costly failure, yet in 1918 Ludendorff decided to risk his entire reserves in a final effort to break the Allied line.

Reasons for Ludendorff's Gamble

(a) The submarine campaign had failed ; Britain could not be starved into submission.
(b) The Allied blockade was undermining the health and morale of the German people.
(c) Germany's allies were giving way under the strain of prolonged war : the Turkish armies were in retreat ; the Bulgarians, having already got all they wanted, were anxious for peace ; the subject peoples of the Austrian Empire naturally faced privation with less fortitude than the Germans.
(d) Reinforcements from the eastern front supplied the means for undertaking an offensive.
(e) It was ' now or never ' ; the American troops were not yet in the field, but would be very shortly.

The March attack on the Somme front broke the British Fifth Army, advanced forty miles, and nearly severed the British link with the French. This Allied disaster brought about the much-needed unification of command, and Foch became the Allied Commander-in-Chief.

The April attack forced the Allies to abandon all the territory so dearly bought in the Passchendaele campaign. The channel ports were seriously threatened.

The May and July attacks drove the French back from the Aisne to the Marne.

There are two explanations for the surprising extent of the German advance. First, instead of attacking in 'waves' of men, they advanced in small groups pressing forward where the opposition was weak and keeping their reserves close at hand to exploit any gap created. Secondly, the British Fifth Army was unusually weak : the line recently taken over from the French had not been put into a proper state of defence ; Haig had massed his reserves in the north, where he expected an attack ; and after Passchendaele, Lloyd George had retained many reserves in England to prevent unprofitable squandering of life. Notwithstanding, the German successes failed to bring victory.

The advances exceeded Ludendorff's expectations, and he was unprepared to exploit them. The British troops offered magnificent resistance in response to Haig's famous order, " With our backs to the wall and believing in the justice of our cause, each one of us must fight on to the end." Finally, the arrival of Allied reserves, in fresh condition from Palestine and Italy, turned the tide.

FOCH'S FINAL OFFENSIVE

On July 15 the last German offensive crossed the Marne, but on July 18 Foch launched a counter-attack against the flank of the salient. This attack was led by masses of light tanks and forced the Germans to retire.

On August 8 (the Black Day of the German Army) Haig attacked in the Somme area. Thanks to the secrecy with which it was prepared and to the tanks which led the assault, this offensive was very successful. When, however, its initial momentum died away, the attack was stopped, for Haig was no longer willing to batter against stiffening opposition. Instead he set in motion the Third Army farther north. This proved a more economical method of attack, and henceforward a series of short, closely related offensives kept the Germans retiring until they reached the Hindenburg line, from which they had started in the spring.

On September 26, with the order, " *Tout le monde à la bataille*," Foch began the final converging battles of the War. The Americans, having flattened out the St Mihiel salient on August 12, advanced northward against Sedan. On August 28 the Belgians and British attacked in the north. Between these two horn-like movements, the Hindenburg line was breached at many points, and the Germans were compelled to make extensive evacuations. The Allied advance, however, was slower than had been expected, and the German army retained its cohesion. Nevertheless, it was sadly pressed, and its fighting spirit was broken. The German soldiers had been led to believe that the Allies were as exhausted and as short of supplies as themselves. During the spring offensives, however, they had captured stores of Allied clothing, food, and metals which opened their eyes to the deception which had been practised upon them. Their casualties had been enormous, and the Allied reserves seemed unlimited. Their letters from home told of their families' distress, and further resistance seemed both hopeless and pointless. After August 8 the Kaiser recognized that they were at the end of their resources and that the War must finish.

The collapse of Germany's Allies soon made matters much worse.

THE GREAT WAR (1914–1918)

Germany's Allies make Peace

I. BULGARIA

While the German army was retiring in France, the Allies at last took the offensive at Salonika, and in a fortnight (September 15 to 29) they overthrew the Bulgars, whose Government made terms with the Allies on September 29.

II. TURKEY

The elimination of Bulgaria exposed both the Danube and Constantinople to attack, and the French and British forces diverged on these two objectives. Turkey, with her armies in the east shattered, made peace on September 30.

III. AUSTRIA

On October 24 an advance was begun on the Italian front, and on October 27 the victory of *Vittorio Veneto* split the Austrian army, which was in disorderly retreat by October 30, when the Government asked for an armistice. This was concluded on November 4.

The Internal Collapse of Germany

The breakdown of Bulgaria on September 29, coming hard upon the launching of Foch's great offensive along the whole length of the western front, broke the nerve of the German High Command. Ludendorff told the political leaders that an armistice was imperative, and Prince Max of Baden was appointed Chancellor to use his international reputation for moderation in the negotiations. On October 3 he requested the President of the United States of America to take in hand the restoration of peace. In the exchange of notes which followed, it became clear that the Allies demanded little short of unconditional surrender. Ludendorff now wished to fight on, but neither the new Government nor the people supported him. Short of proper clothing and fuel, weakened by semi-starvation and racked by the influenza epidemic which killed 1722 people in Berlin on one day (October 15), they demanded peace and turned on the leaders who had promised them victory and brought defeat. Ludendorff was dismissed, and steps were taken to transfer the real power to the Reichstag, for President Wilson had refused to enter into negotiations with " monarchical autocrats." Civil war was threatened, for the Kaiser, despite relentless pressure, was unwilling to abdicate. On October 29 he left Berlin for Spa, the army headquarters, where Hindenburg had to tell him that the army would not support him against the people. On the same day mutiny broke out in the navy. Ordered to put out to sea, the sailors refused. By November 4 the mutiny was general, and Kiel was in the hands of the mutineers. The same day the army fell into confusion in Flanders, and the Austrian armistice exposed the Bavarian frontier to hostile attack. A few days later the mutineers had occupied the principal cities of North-west Germany, and insurrection had broken out in Munich. On November 9 revolutionaries occupied the streets of Berlin. A Republic was proclaimed from the steps of the Reichstag, and, at last bowing to the inevitable, the Kaiser fled to Holland. On November 7 the German delegates had passed through the Allied lines to receive the terms drawn up

MAP 26

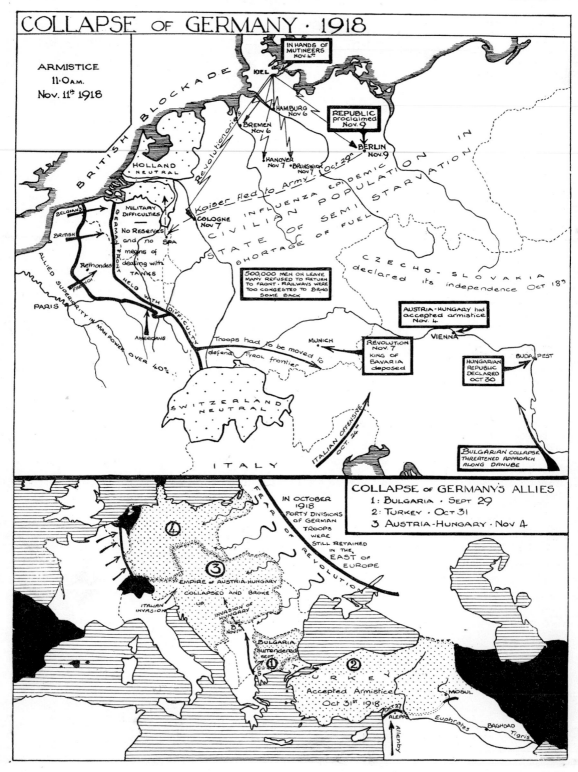

COLLAPSE of GERMANY · 1918

ARMISTICE
11·0 A.M.
Nov. 11ᵗʰ 1918

IN HANDS OF
MUTINEERS
NOV. 4ᵗʰ

KIEL

BRITISH BLOCKADE

HAMBURG
Nov 6

BREMEN
Nov 6

REPUBLIC
proclaimed
Nov. 9

BERLIN
Nov. 9

HOLLAND
NEUTRAL

HANOVER
Nov 7

BRUNSWICK
Nov 7

Kaiser fled to Army Oct 29ᵗʰ

COLOGNE
Nov 7

Revolutionaries

INFLUENZA EPIDEMIC IN
CIVILIAN POPULATION IN
STATE OF SEMI-STARVATION
SHORTAGE OF FUEL.

CZECHO-
SLOVAKIA
declared its independence Oct 18ᵗʰ

BELGIANS

BRITISH

Rethondes

MILITARY
DIFFICULTIES
No Reserves
and no
means of
dealing with
TANKS

GERMAN RETREAT HELD WITH DIFFICULTY

PARIS

ALLIED SUPERIORITY IN MAN POWER OVER 40%

FRENCH

AMERICANS

500,000 MEN ON LEAVE
MANY REFUSED TO RETURN
TO FRONT. RAILWAYS WERE
TOO CONGESTED TO BRING
SOME BACK

AUSTRIA-HUNGARY had
accepted armistice
Nov. 4

VIENNA

Troops had to be moved to
defend Tyrol frontier

MUNICH

REVOLUTION
NOV. 7
KING
OF
BAVARIA
deposed

HUNGARIAN
REPUBLIC
DECLARED
OCT 30

BUDA PEST

SWITZERLAND
NEUTRAL

ITALIAN OFFENSIVE OCT 24ᵗʰ

ITALY

BULGARIAN COLLAPSE
THREATENED APPROACH
ALONG DANUBE

IN OCTOBER
1918
FORTY DIVISIONS
OF GERMAN
TROOPS
WERE
STILL RETAINED
IN THE
EAST OF
EUROPE

FEAR OF REVOLUTION

COLLAPSE of GERMANY'S ALLIES
1: BULGARIA · SEPT 29
2: TURKEY · OCT 31
3 AUSTRIA-HUNGARY · NOV 4

①

③
EMPIRE OF AUSTRIA-HUNGARY
COLLAPSED AND BROKE
UP.

ITALIAN
INVASION

INVASION
OF
HUNGARY
B
NOV IIᵗʰ

Bulgaria
Surrendered
Sept.

①

②
TURKEY
Accepted Armistice
Oct 31ˢᵗ 1918

MOSUL

OCT 27
ALEPPO

Allenby

Euphrates

BAGHDAD
Tigris

by the Allied Commanders. On November 11, 1918, they were forced to agree to the stringent Allied terms, and at 11 o'clock on that morning the Great War came to an end.

The Russian Revolution

I. CZARIST *RÉGIME*

At the end of the nineteenth century the Russian Government was the most completely autocratic in Europe. It was also the weakest and the most oppressive. The arbitrary rule of the Czar was imposed on his subjects through an army of corrupt officials, whose inefficiency aroused formidable opposition among the educated classes. Only the activities of the secret police enabled the established order to survive, for secret revolutionary forces were at work in Russia long before the outbreak of the Great War.

II. GROWTH OF OPPOSITION

(a) *The Liberals*, drawn in the main from the enlightened nobility and professional classes, clamoured for reforms and chiefly for the summoning of a representative assembly (the Duma).

(b) *The Socialists*, followers of Karl Marx, wanted to set up a new order of society in which the workers would control the means of production and the distribution of wealth. There was a schism in their party : the moderates were prepared to co-operate with the Liberals to secure their ends by gradual means ; the extremists (called Bolsheviks) wanted to seize power by revolution.

(c) *The Terrorists*, most of whom were university students, were prepared to go to any lengths to overthrow the Government.

(d) Opposition also came from oppressed nationalities, like the Poles and the Finns, who resented their subjection to the Russian Czar.

The leaders of these active political movements sought the support of the peasants and the factory-workers, whose miserable lot made them fertile soil for the revolutionary seed.

The Peasants were hostile to the impoverished landowners. The emancipation of the serfs in 1861 had reduced the estates and the influence of the landowners, who had neither the initiative nor the capital to develop the estates that remained to them after the peasants were freed. They held fast to their land and took little interest in local affairs.

The lot of the peasants was appalling : they were badly housed and barely able to eke out a living with their primitive agriculture. The land which they had gained in 1861 was of low productivity ; it was held in common by the village community and divided annually. As the population grew, conditions became worse, because the holdings were multiplied. When the harvest was bad the peasants starved. They therefore supported those who would give them what they wanted—land.

The Factory-workers. At the end of the nineteenth century Russia was rapidly industrialized. Factories grew up in the larger towns, and round them developed slums in which the workers lived. Both housing- and factory-conditions were indescribably bad, and the Government did little to improve either.

The general strike of 1905 was one of several organized by the Social-Democrats

MAP 27

REVOLUTIONS IN RUSSIA

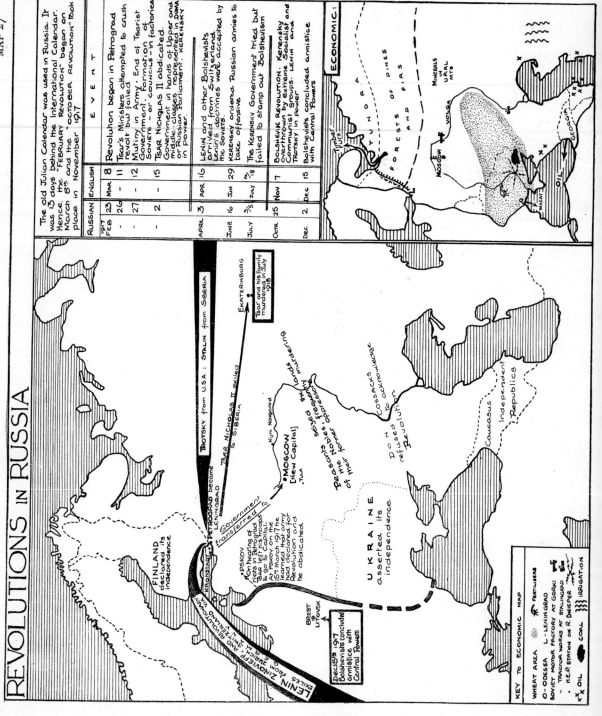

The old Julian Calendar was used in Russia. It was 13 days behind the International Calendar. Hence, the "FEBRUARY REVOLUTION" began on March 8th and the "OCTOBER REVOLUTION" took place in November 1917.

RUSSIAN	ENGLISH		E V E N T
1917 FEB	23	MAR. 8	Revolution began in Petrograd
-	26	- 11	Tsar's Ministers attempted to crush revolt but failed
-	27	- 12	Mutiny in Army. End of Tsarist Government. Formation of Soviets - or councils - in factories
-	2	- 15	Tsar Nicholas II abdicated. Government in hands of Upper and middle classes represented in DUMA or Russian Parliament. KERENSKY in power.
APRIL	3	APR. 16	Lenin and other Bolshevists arrived from Switzerland. Lenin's doctrines were accepted by the Soviets.
JUNE	16	JUN. 29	Kerensky ordered Russian armies to take offensive
JULY	3/5	JULY 14/18	The Kerensky Government tried but failed to stamp out Bolshevism
OCT.	25	NOV. 7	BOLSHEVIK REVOLUTION. Kerensky overthrown by extreme Socialist Communist groups. LENIN and TROTSKY in power
DEC.	2	DEC. 15	Bolshevists concluded armistice with Central Powers

ECONOMIC:

TRISHEN FOREST OF PINES AND FIRS

TUNDRA

MINERALS IN URAL MTS

MOSCOW

VOLGA

OIL

WHEAT

GEORGIA

FINLAND declared its independence

PETROGRAD become LENINGRAD

KRONSTADT

PSKOV. On hearing of riots in Petrograd Tsar left his troops to go to Capital. At Pskov on the 15ᵗʰ March 1917, he learned that army had declared for Revolution and he abdicated.

Government transferred to

●MOSCOW [New Capital]
.TULA

LENIN ZINOVIEFF AND REVOLUTION 1917 RETURN FROM EXILES

BREST LITOVSK

Dec 15ᵗʰ 1917 Bolshevists concluded armistice with Central Powers

TROTSKY from U.S.A : STALIN from SIBERIA

TSAR NICHOLAS II exiled to SIBERIA

Nijni Novgorod

Peasants seized the lands frequently murdering the Nobles, oppressors of their former

EKATERINBURG

Tsar and his family murdered in July 1918

DON COSSACKS refused to acknowledge Revolution

UKRAINE asserted its independence

Caucasus Independent Republics

KEY TO ECONOMIC MAP

WHEAT AREA
O-ODESSA L-LENINGRAD FERTILISERS
SOVIET MOTOR FACTORY AT GORKI
- TRACTOR WORKS AT STALINGRAD
- H.E.P. STATION ON R. DNIEPER
xˣx OIL ●COAL ⌇⌇⌇ IRRIGATION

(Socialist Party) who realized that the workers could more readily be won to their point of view than the peasants.

III. THE WAR

The Russian Government was quite unable to cope with the task of conducting a great war. Russia, still predominantly agricultural, had to contend against Germany, the most powerful industrial country in Europe. Against the German big guns the Russian troops were in effect unarmed. Lack of adequate communications made it difficult for the original supplies of imported weapons to be replaced. The efforts made to increase the output of military supplies in Russia only dislocated the normal production of necessities. The demands of military transport and bad weather disorganized the distribution of foodstuffs. Thus discontent was rife both in the army and at home.

Nicholas was a weak and ineffective man surrounded by evil counsellors like the monk Rasputin. Neither he nor his advisers were capable of dealing with the crisis which arose.

IV. THE EVENTS OF 1917

In March, 1917, a strike broke out in Petrograd, and the workers set up administrative councils called *Soviets*. Soldiers called to disperse the crowds joined forces with them. On March 15 the Czar, having no supporters, was forced to abdicate at Pskov. He was subsequently murdered with his family at Ekaterinburg while on his way to exile in Siberia.

A provisional Government of the Liberals and moderate Socialists was installed, and Kerensky took control. Real power, however, rested with the Soviets. Kerensky attempted to continue the War, but this was impossible. The heart of the revolution was anti-War, and in any case over a million men had deserted in March to go home and take part in the prospective distribution of land. Kerensky put down several attempts against the nominal Government, but the Bolsheviks, Lenin and Trotsky, who had returned to Russia, were skilfully plotting to overthrow him. The failure of the Government troops against a renewed German offensive strengthened the Bolsheviks. They secured a majority in the Soviets, and on November 7 (October 25, old style) the provisional Government was overthrown and Russia became the ' Russian Socialist Federal Soviet Republic.'

V. THE TREATY OF BREST LITOVSK

The Bolsheviks were opposed to the War, which they regarded as being purely imperialist and capitalist. They also needed peace for the internal reconstruction of Russia. Immediately, therefore, upon their accession to power they made proposals for an armistice to all countries. When the Allies, who did not recognize the new Government, failed to reply, Russia proceeded to negotiate a separate peace. The Bolsheviks believed that a settlement could be made on the basis of " No annexations and no indemnities." The Central Powers appeared to accept this principle, but it soon became clear that they did not intend to be deprived of the fruits of their victory. General Hoffmann pointed out that Russia was now impotent and dictated terms of great harshness. Map 28 shows the territories detached from Russia.

MAP 28

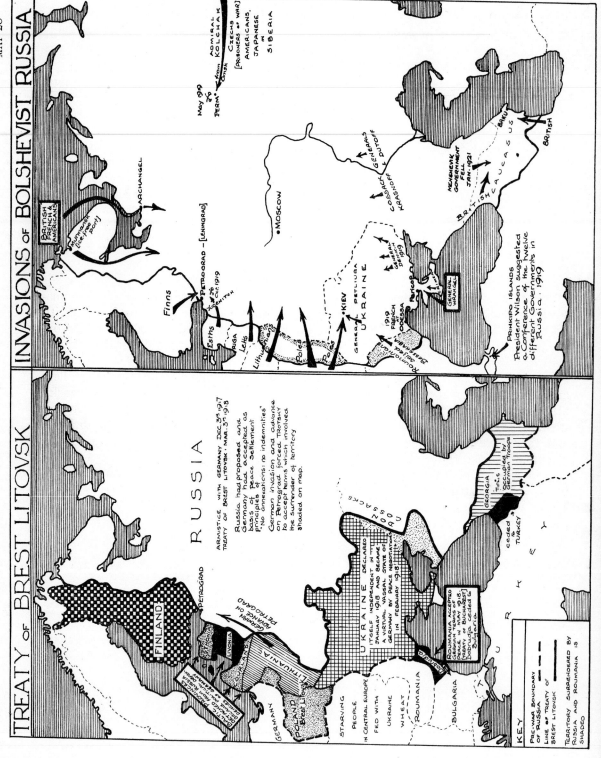

TREATY of BREST LITOVSK

INVASIONS of BOLSHEVIST RUSSIA

RUSSIA

ARMISTICE with GERMANY · DEC. 3rd 1917
TREATY of BREST LITOVSK · MAR. 3rd 1918

Russia had proposed and
Germany had accepted as
basis of Peace Settlement
principles of
"No annexations: no indemnities"

German invasion and advance
on Petrograd forced Trotsky
to accept terms which involved
the surrender of territory
shaded on map.

FINLAND

PETROGRAD

Germany advance on Petrograd

ESTHONIA
LIVONIA
COURLAND
LITHUANIA
POLAND Brest Litovsk

GERMANY

STARVING PEOPLE
IN CENTRAL EUROPE
FED WITH
UKRAINE
WHEAT

UKRAINE DECLARED
ITSELF INDEPENDENT IN
JANUARY 1918 AND BECAME
A VIRTUAL VASSAL STATE OF
GERMANY BY PEACE NEGOTIATIONS
IN FEBRUARY 1918

COSSACKS

GEORGIA
Tiflis occupied by German Troops

ROUMANIA ACCEPTED
GERMAN TERMS OF
PEACE IN MAY 1918
(TREATY of BUCHAREST)
Dobrudja ceded to
Bulgaria.

ROUMANIA
BULGARIA

ceded by TURKEY

T U R K E Y

KEY

PRE-WAR BOUNDARY OF RUSSIA
LINE of TREATY of BREST LITOVSK

TERRITORY SURRENDERED BY RUSSIA AND ROUMANIA IS SHADED

BRITISH FRENCH & AMERICANS

Murmansk [ice-free port]

ARCHANGEL

Finns

Esths
Letts
Lithuania

PETROGRAD – [LENINGRAD]
General Yudenitch Oct. 1919

RIGA

Poles

General Petlura
KIEV
UKRAINE

MOSCOW

Revolutions among Russian Peasants

1919 FRENCH at ODESSA

GENERAL WRANGEL

GENERAL DENIKIN 1919

COSSACK GENERAL KRASNOFF

COSSACK GENERALS DUTOFF

MENSHEVIK GOVERNMENT FELL JAN. 1921

BAKU

BRITISH CAUCASUS
CAUCASUS U.S.
BRITISH

May 199 PERM from OMSK
ADMIRAL KOLCHAK

CZECHS [PRISONERS of WAR]
AMERICANS,
JAPANESE
in SIBERIA

PRINKIPO ISLANDS
President Wilson suggested
a Conference of the twelve
different Governments in
Russia. 1919

At first Trotsky, the leader of the Russian delegation, refused to submit. The result was a new German invasion, which came within a hundred miles of Petrograd. Lenin, the President of the Congress of Soviets, was then able to persuade his associates to agree, and the treaty was signed on March 2, 1918.

VI. INVASIONS OF SOVIET RUSSIA

In the months that followed the signing of the treaty, Russia was confronted by military invasions from all quarters, and great confusion prevailed.

Despite her aversion to Bolshevism, Germany took little part in these invasions, for she regarded the new Government as the one least likely to menace German interests. German soldiers, however, were sent to Finland to support the anti-Bolshevists ; German troops penetrated the Ukraine in large numbers to secure the harvest of grain which was required to save the Central Powers from starvation.

The Allied Governments disliked the new *régime*. To people preoccupied with the prosecution of the War, the Bolsheviks appeared to be German agents. Their Communist propaganda made them more objectionable in the eyes of some people than the Germans themselves. With mixed motives, therefore, the Allies dispatched military expeditions which assisted the 'White' armies of counter-revolutionaries. In 1920, following a Polish invasion of the Ukraine, the army of 'Red' Russia advanced against Warsaw but was defeated at the 'miracle of the Vistula.' The hero of this battle was Pilsudski, who later became the dictator of Poland. The dispatch of the French general, Weygand, to advise the Poles reflected the general hatred and fear inspired in western Europe by the bogey of Bolshevism. With the defeat of General Wrangel at Pericop in 1920, and the overthrow of the Menshevik [1] Government in Georgia the following January, the Soviets put an end to 'White' opposition in the west. The foreign troops were withdrawn, but counter-revolutions in Siberia were not suppressed till some years later.

---

[1] Menshevik, the less extreme Socialists.

MAP 29

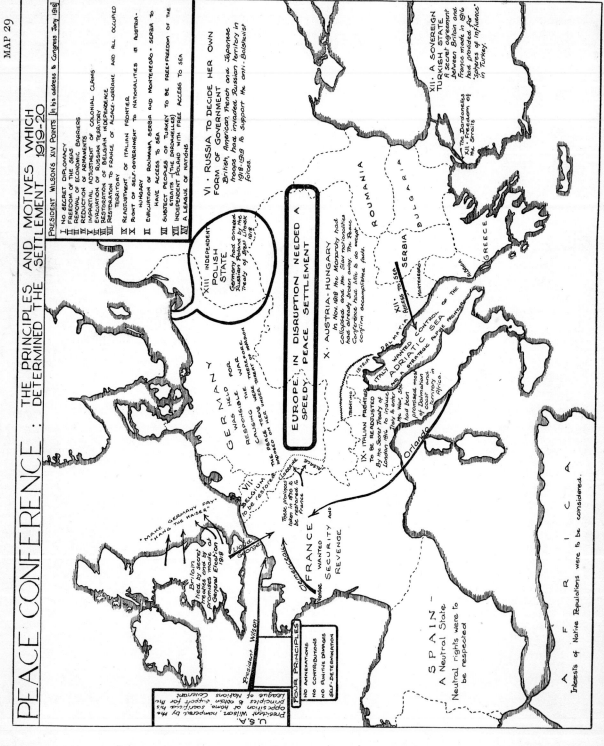

PEACE CONFERENCE: THE PRINCIPLES AND MOTIVES WHICH DETERMINED THE SETTLEMENT 1919-20

THE PEACE CONFERENCE OF PARIS (1919)

Principles and Motives which determined the Settlement

On November 11, 1918, an armistice was accepted by Germany. It brought to an end a bitter struggle which had encompassed the nations of the earth for four years. Now the statesmen were confronted with the difficult task, not merely of reconstructing the boundaries of Europe, but of establishing a world peace settlement.

The armistice terms imposed by the Allies were severe and left Germany prostrate. She surrendered her guns and fleet and withdrew her armies from conquered territory. The German Government accepted the terms, because the Allies at the same time made a solemn promise that the principles which President Wilson of the U.S.A. had set forth should form the basis of the peace settlement.

I. PURPOSE OF THE PEACE CONFERENCE OF PARIS

The purpose of the statesmen was to plan the details of the settlement, the basis of which (the 'Fourteen Points') had already been agreed upon.

(a) The Fourteen Points

If the Allies wanted a stable peace, it had to be founded on justice. The ideals presented by President Wilson appeared to satisfy this requirement; if carried into effect, they would have been the surest road to 'a world safe for democracy' envisaged by democratic statesmen.

The most important of the Fourteen Points were:

(i) That secret diplomatic arrangements which had been largely responsible for the outbreak of the War should be set aside in favour of "open covenants of peace openly arrived at."

(ii) That economic barriers—the setting up of high tariff walls and the restriction of trade—should be broken down.

(iii) That nations must reduce armaments.

(iv) That the settlement must satisfy the national aspirations of the peoples of the world, and that the needs of backward peoples should be safeguarded.

(v) That no severe penalties should be imposed on the defeated.

(vi) That there should be established a League of Nations with a Covenant aimed at securing international co-operation towards peace. This was President Wilson's greatest constructive suggestion.

II. MAKERS OF THE PEACE TREATIES

All the Allies were invited to the Peace Conference which met at Paris in January, 1919, but important decisions were made by the 'Big Four'—President Wilson of the U.S.A., Clemenceau of France, Mr Lloyd George, and Signor Orlando of Italy.

Wilson, the American, whose ideals were the hope of victors and vanquished alike, was sincerely anxious to carry out his promises. He lost influence because he had few practical plans to offer upon which his ideals of a just settlement could be built. In diplomatic skill he was not the equal of the other statesmen. Because he believed that the establishment of the League of Nations was the only hope of permanent world peace, he was led to compromise on matters where the views of the practical statesmen conflicted with the ideals of his fourteen points in order to secure their acceptance of the Covenant. Moreover, he had the support only of a minority of Americans; those who upheld the traditional policy of non-interventon in European affairs were hostile to him. Opposition at home weakened his prestige at the Conference. The Senate of the U.S.A. refused to ratify his work, and at the election following the treaties he was not re-elected President.

Clemenceau, the Prime Minister of France and Chairman of the Peace Conference, was a realist. He had no faith in Wilson's ideals. He knew exactly what he wanted— to crush Germany while he had the chance. He regarded Franco-German hostility as natural and inevitable. Had Germany won, she would not have spared France. Now that she had been utterly defeated, he had the opportunity he desired—to destroy her power to threaten the security of France. He worked for France and France alone. Nothing else interested him. He dominated the conference. His uncompromising attitude earned for him the epithet, 'Tiger.' His policy triumphed because his influence weakened the forces making for an ideal peace.

Mr Lloyd George, the English Prime Minister, recognized the necessity for a peace which would satisfy Germany and restore her prosperity. He personally favoured moderate terms, but gave only limited support to Wilson's views because (a) Britain, like France, was bound by treaties concluded during the War for the satisfaction of her Allies at the expense of the defeated, (b) he was bound by his election-pledges of 1918, in which he had promised to demand penalties from the enemy. While France sought military security, Britain eliminated a commercial rival by destroying the German fleet, the German Mercantile Marine, and the German Empire.

Signor Orlando, the Italian representative, had less influence. He was bent on securing for Italy an expansion of territory. He was interested only in discussions which concerned the satisfaction of Italy's ambitions.

III. DIFFICULTIES WHICH BESET THE PEACE-MAKERS

(a) Europe was in confusion. Old empires had fallen; new nations had already set up Governments. Starvation and disease aggravated the horrors resulting from war. The statesmen were forced to act quickly.

(b) *The Secret Agreements* (*see Maps* 41 *and* 44).

(c) One of the difficulties experienced by democratic statesmen is that they have to consider not only what they believe ought to be done, but also what their electorate demands. Neither Mr Lloyd George nor President Wilson was a free agent.

(d) Paris was an unfortunate choice for a peace conference, as the passions of the people were inflamed by close contact with the War and its miseries. Statesmen could not free themselves from the tense atmosphere which prevailed.

The peace treaties which resulted reflected the spirit of the conference, in which were represented opposing forces demanding (a) the rewards of victory, (b) the magnanimous settlement of conflicting claims designed to secure permanent peace.

The result was a decisive triumph for (*a*), but the influence (*b*) was not completely lost. On the one hand there was no open discussion, and the main points of the settlement were secretly decided by the ' Big Four.' The defeated Powers were disarmed, but the victors maintained their military strength. In spite of Wilson's principles, penal clauses were added to the treaties. On the other hand it may be claimed that the map of Europe was redrawn to correspond with national divisions, and the Covenant of the League of Nations seemed to be a definite step towards international peace.

The most satisfactory post-War settlement was the Treaty of Lausanne with Turkey for the following reasons : (*a*) it was made in 1923, when the bitterness of war had somewhat subsided ; (*b*) it was made in a neutral town, where the problems could be more dispassionately reviewed ; (*c*) it was made between the Allies and Turkey, when the latter had recovered from the humiliation and weakness of overwhelming defeat.

The Main Features of the Peace Settlement

I. THE TREATIES

(*a*) Separate treaties were concluded with each of the defeated countries : St Germain, with Austria, in 1919 ; Trianon, with Hungary, in 1921 ; Neuilly, with Bulgaria, in 1919. All these were modelled upon the Treaty of Versailles, signed with Germany in 1919.

The Covenant of the League formed the first part of each treaty, and then followed territorial changes and disarmament clauses. Reparations were exacted from Germany alone ; she had to undertake to pay the cost of the War, as her Allies were bankrupt.

MAP 30

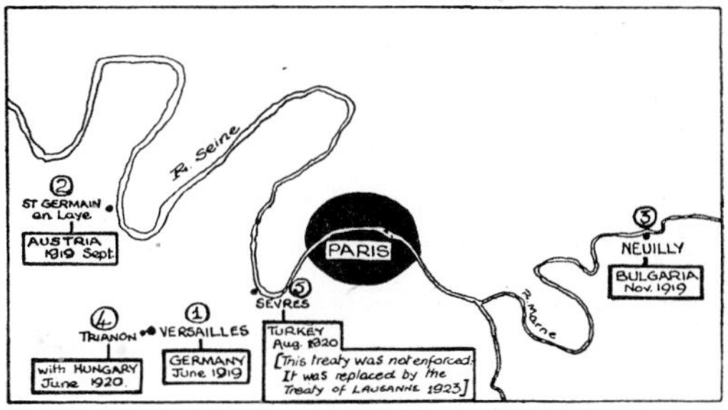

PARIS: INDEX TO THE PEACE TREATIES

(*b*) The final settlement with Turkey was not completed until 1923, by the Treaty of Lausanne.

(*c*) The map of Europe was also altered by treaties concluded between the U.S.S.R. and the former Baltic Provinces of Russia.

II. TERRITORIAL CHANGES

Map 31 illustrates the New Europe which resulted from these arrangements.

(*a*) All the Allies, except America, gained territory as a result of the dismemberment of the German, Austrian, and Turkish Empires.

(i) *France* regained Alsace-Lorraine.

(ii) *Britain, France*, and *Japan* gained colonial territories. (See Map 36.)

(iii) *Italy* gained the Trentino, part of South Tyrol, and part of Dalmatia.

(iv) *Serbia* was united to *Montenegro*, to which was added Bosnia and Herzegovina, Croatia, parts of Styria, and Dalmatia. The new state was called Yugoslavia.

(v) *Greece* gained further territories in Macedonia. (Thrace and part of Asia Minor, originally given to Greece, were lost by the Treaty of Lausanne. See Map 44.)

63

MAP 31

EUROPE SHOWING THE MAIN FEATURES OF THE PEACE SETTLEMENT

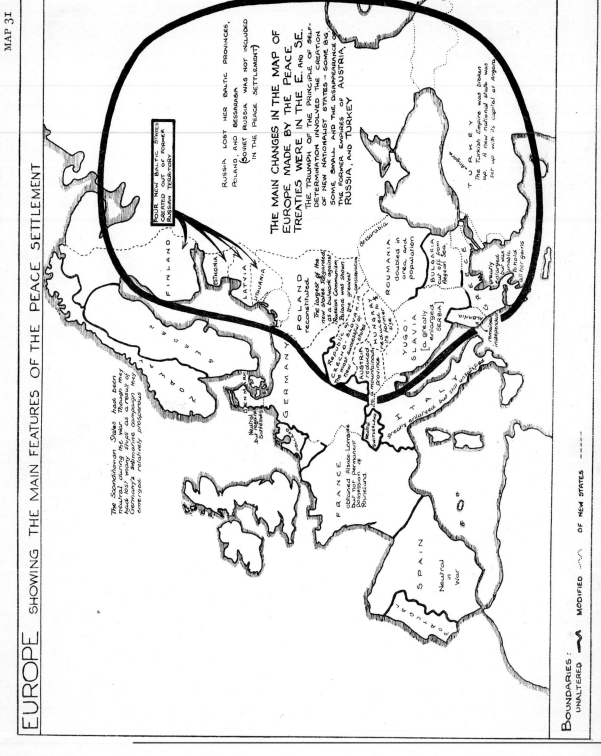

BOUNDARIES: UNALTERED ———   MODIFIED ∿∿∿   OF NEW STATES ------

(vi) *Roumania* gained Bessarabia, Transylvania, and the Banat of Temesvar.

(*b*) Six new states were set up :

   (i) Poland.

   (ii) Czecho-Slovakia.

   (iii) Finland ⎫

   (iv) Esthonia ⎪

   (v) Latvia ⎬ originally Russian territory.

   (vi) Lithuania ⎭

III. CHARACTERISTICS OF THE NEW EUROPE

(*a*) *The Impotence of Germany*

Germany, before the War the most powerful and progressive nation in Europe, was reduced to impotence economically and politically by the peace. Her security was threatened by the disarmament clauses, her economic life by demands for reparations. This loss of national prestige and prosperity by a great nation was dangerous to the permanent settlement of Europe. Germany is a Central European Power, and any problem of importance in Europe affects her.

(*b*) *The Ascendancy of France in Europe*

France once more assumed the leading position on the Continent to which Europe had been accustomed before the rise of Germany. France, however, had not defeated Germany by her own efforts but by the united strength of her wartime Allies. Her dominant position in Europe is still dependent on external support.

(*c*) *The Insignificance of Post-War Austria*

From the ruins of the old Hapsburg Empire there emerged the small republic of Austria, a mountainous area in the Alps, with a huge capital, Vienna, all that was left of its traditional greatness. Reduced by disease and starvation, its very existence threatened, Austria was one of the first states whose difficulties engaged the attention of the statesmen of Europe after the War.

(*d*) *The Rise of Italy*

As one of the chief Allies in the War, Italy gained a leading position among the Powers. Nevertheless, the Italians were gravely dissatisfied ; they felt that their national greatness had not been recognized. The rise of Italy has changed the ' balance of power ' in the Mediterranean Sea.

(*e*) *The Transformation of Russia*

The Revolution which swept away the Tsarist *régime* resulted in the formation of a Union of Socialist Republics, and this new Russia, absorbed in the task of creating a new economic state, withdrew from active participation in the affairs of Europe.

(*f*) *The Increased Importance of Small States*

As a result of the Peace Settlement there are many more small states in Europe than there were before the War. The League of Nations gave them their opportunity to co-operate and thus to influence the decisions of the Great Powers.

E

MAP 32

GERMANY'S LOSSES

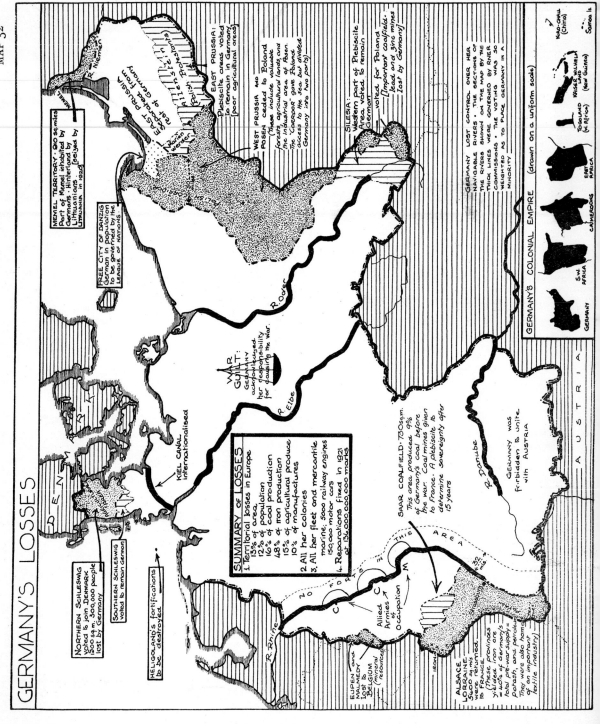

(g) *The Growth of Economic Nationalism in the Danubian Area*

The frontiers of the countries in the Danube Basin were settled upon national lines. There now exists a group of aggressively national states which aim at securing economic as well as political independence, a situation dangerous alike to the prosperity and peace of Europe. Jealous of their neighbours and fearful of their former ruling peoples, the Germans of Austria and the Magyars of Hungary, they are strengthening their military resources.

(h) *The Spread of Democratic Forms of Government*

The War appeared to be a decisive victory for democracy. Democratic republics now replaced the autocratic empires of Hohenzollern, Hapsburg, and Romanoff. But new influences soon undermined the stability of these Parliamentary Governments; in the rival doctrines of Communism and Fascism representative institutions were scorned.

GERMANY'S LOSSES

Map 32 is designed to illustrate (a) the territorial, and (b) the economic losses of Germany in Europe.

Germany was condemned by the Peace Conference for the responsibility of her former rulers in causing the War. It seemed natural to a war-suffering Europe that Germany should be punished for her crime. War had caused destruction and loss of property, and the Allied statesmen demanded recompense. This point of view was held by Clemenceau, the French statesman, who, in his desire for the security of his own country, was anxious to weaken Germany so that she could no longer prove dangerous to her neighbour.

Two motives dictated the terms of peace: (a) to punish Germany; (b) to weaken Germany to a point where she could no longer cause trouble.

One of the most unpopular and unjust clauses of the treaty was the " War Guilt Clause," which forced Germany in spite of protests to acknowledge her guilt. The belief of the Allies that Germany alone was responsible for the War justified, in their eyes, her punishment.

In addition to the territorial and economic losses of Germany there were the disarmament clauses of the treaty, which, by reducing her army and destroying her navy, rendered the position of Germany in Europe impotent and relegated her to the rank of a secondary state. The provinces of Germany west of the Rhine were demilitarized—no forts were to be built and no troops permitted to enter—and an Allied army of occupation was also forced upon her.

I. TERRITORIAL LOSSES

While the Austrian and Turkish Empires were broken up, the German Empire was not so drastically partitioned, chiefly because fewer alien nationalities lived under her sovereignty. She lost, however, all her colonies. Many thousands of German citizens were transferred to the rule of neighbouring states.

The most important losses in Europe were the provinces of *Alsace-Lorraine*, which were restored to France. The provinces of *West Prussia* and *Posen* were transferred

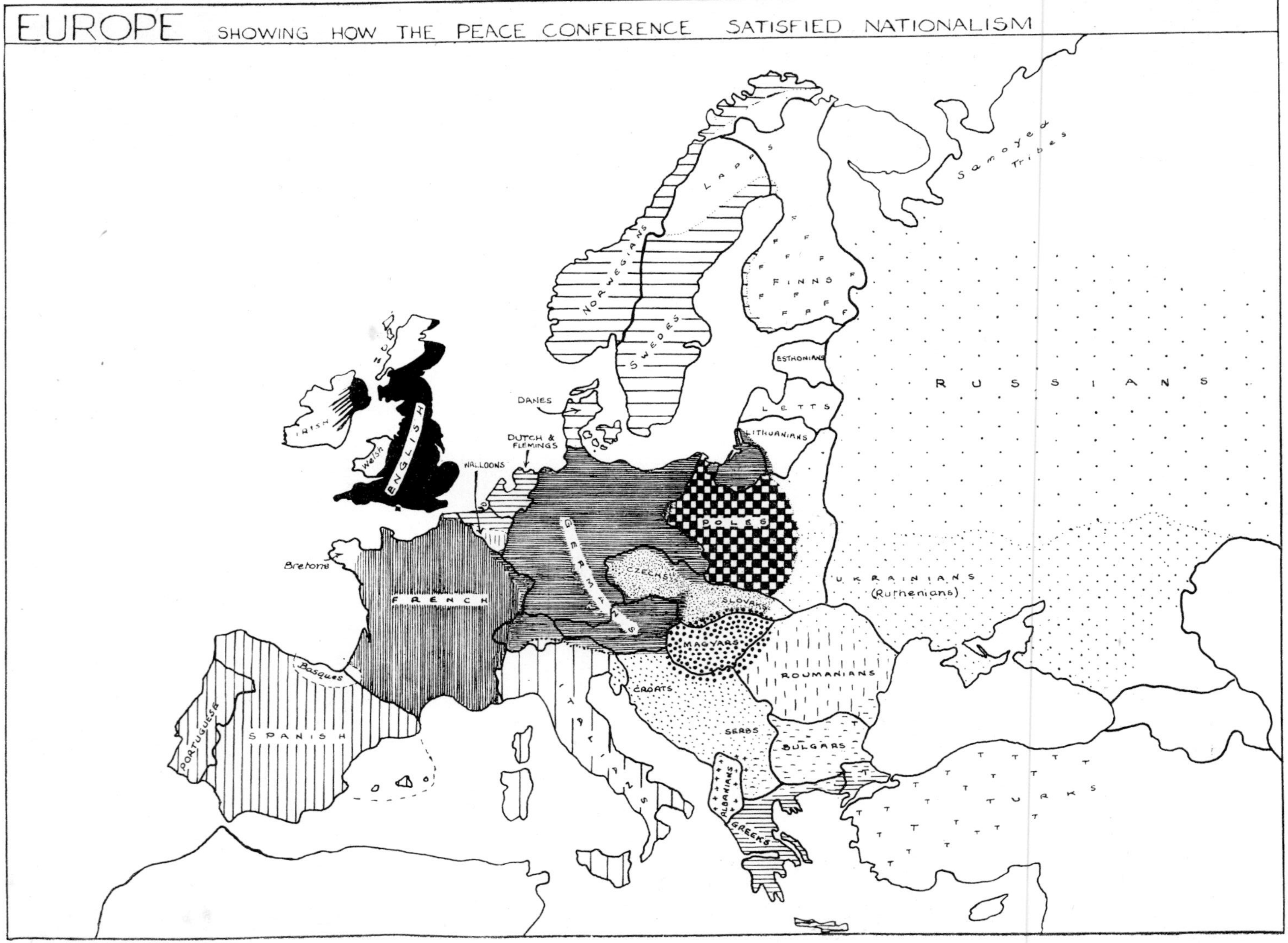

MAP 33

EUROPE

SHOWING HOW THE PEACE CONFERENCE SATISFIED NATIONALISM

to Poland, in order to afford this new state access to the Baltic. This proposal aroused the strongest opposition, because it divided Germany into two parts. The decision to place the purely German city of *Danzig* under the control of the League of Nations, out of consideration for the Polish demand that Germany should not control the mouth of their great River Vistula, also caused great dissatisfaction. The loss of part of *Upper Silesia*, though small in area, was of great economic importance. *Memelland* had a population of Lithuanians, though in the port of Memel itself there was a German majority. Minor adjustments of frontier to Germany's disadvantage took place on the Danish frontier in *Schleswig* and on the Belgian frontier at *Eupen* and *Malmedy*.

France wanted all the territory up to the left bank of the Rhine, but all the other Allies refused to concede this demand, preferring to guarantee her security in less objectionable ways.

II. ECONOMIC LOSSES

These territorial losses alone were sufficient to create a sense of injustice in the minds of the Germans, but the effect of the economic provisions of the treaty was to convince them that the Allies were bent on their total ruin.

The prosperity of Germany depended on her industrial and commercial development. The territorial annexations had taken away from her valuable mineral resources as well as fully grown industrial enterprises, *e.g.*, the textile-mills of Alsace. Not content with this, the Allies proceeded to imperil what remained by demanding reparations in the form of coal, the cession of railway stock, and her mercantile marine ; they interfered with her control over her navigable rivers and took away the special rights she had obtained in Morocco, Egypt, and China.

The effect of all these arrangements was to ruin Germany economically, and since all nations are mutually dependent, they caused economic distress throughout Europe.

Reparations were to be paid in recompense for damage done to civilians in the Allied countries where the fighting had taken place. This additional drain upon the economic resources of Germany is more fully considered on pp. 83–87.

The Attempt to satisfy Nationalist Aspirations

The task of the Allied statesmen was difficult. They had to redraw the map of Europe in accordance with the wishes of the people. In former treaties, *e.g.*, at Vienna in 1815, the statesmen had to consider only the claims of the rulers.

A rapid glance at Map 33 is sufficient to show that a serious attempt was made in 1919 to arrange the frontiers of the states so that the main boundaries coincided with the national divisions of the European peoples. As a result of the treaties, only a small minority (3 per cent.) are still under the subjection of other races. In many cases the peoples themselves had taken the initiative and proclaimed their independence —the peacemakers had to accept what had already been accomplished. Their task was to fix the new boundaries of these groups.

In the main, Poles, Czechs, Roumanians, Serbs, and Greeks had every reason to be satisfied with the treatment they received.

A SKETCH-MAP HISTORY OF THE GREAT WAR AND AFTER

I. NEWLY FORMED NATIONAL STATES

(a) *Poland*

The Poles are a people of Slav race, but of Roman Catholic religion.

Though divided for a century, they had never ceased to resist their conquerors, and they speedily asserted their independence on the collapse of their oppressors. They were generously supported at the conference. Clemenceau welcomed the renaissance of Poland as a bulwark against Germany and Russia, and Wilson had proclaimed at the outset that it was the duty of European statesmen to assist the Poles.

(b) *Czecho-Slovakia*

This country is peopled by Czechs and Slovaks—both Slav peoples.

The Czechs, a cultured people long oppressed, had nevertheless resisted their Austrian masters in the nineteenth century. France realized that the position of their land made the northern Slavs a strategic position in Central Europe—a barrier against possible Austrian and Hungarian aggression. President Wilson was impressed by the Czech leaders, who welcomed the setting-up of the League of Nations enthusiastically. He was probably influenced by the fact that the Czechs, like the Poles, formed an important minority of the population of the U.S.A.

II. PRE-WAR STATES ENLARGE

(a) *Roumania*

This country is peopled by a Latin race of Roman Catholic religion.

Roumania had taken the advantage of the weakness of Hungary to seize Transylvania, and of the preoccupation of Russia to take possession of Bessarabia ; at the Peace Conference she successfully asserted her claims to these provinces on the grounds that Roumanian people were in the majority. In many parts of these new territories the races are very mixed, and the difficulty of a fairer apportionment of the lands proved insuperable. In the Southern Dobrudja, however, there was unquestionably a Bulgarian majority ; nevertheless, this territory remained in Roumania's hands.

(b) *Serbia*

This country is peopled by Southern Slavs.

The Serbs were enabled to satisfy their desire to unite with the Croats and Slovenes after the break-up of the Austro-Hungarian Empire. All these people were of kindred Slav race, though the Croats were Roman Catholics while the Serbs were of the Greek Orthodox faith. Wilson supported the claims of the Southern Slavs against Italy, to whom the Allies had promised the lands along the Dalmatian coast, which was peopled by the Slavs. Clemenceau also agreed with Wilson, not because he was interested in the ideal of satisfying the national aspirations of the Slav peoples, but because it afforded a practical method of detaching the provinces from Austria without the dangerous necessity of transferring them to Italy.

(c) *Greece*

Greece was allotted territory generously at the expense of Turkey in Macedonia, Thrace, and Asia Minor because of the forceful influence of the Greek Prime Minister, Venizelos, who exaggerated the importance of the maritime Greek populations in the coastal towns of the Ægean Sea.   In her war with Turkey (1921–1922) most of these additions were lost.   (See Map 44.)

(d) Baltic States ; Finland ; Esthonia ; Latvia ; Lithuania

These non-Slav peoples had lived unhappily under the rule of the Russian Czar. They also had asserted their independence after the outbreak of the Russian Revolution in 1917, and it was recognized by Germany in the Treaty of Brest Litovsk (see Map 28). The frontiers of these newly formed states were not settled at the Peace Conference, but by arrangement with the U.S.S.R.

III. VICTIMS OF THE PEACE SETTLEMENT

For the first time in modern history Europe was divided on national lines, yet there were many injustices to minorities, especially to those who lived in the defeated countries.   In criticizing the arrangements it should be remembered that the Allied statesmen were faced by an almost impossible task.

People of different nationalities, especially in the south-east of Europe, were inextricably intermingled ; a great number of different solutions of the problems, apparently equally just, was possible.

Frontiers which would enable a nation to have a chance of economic existence had to be devised.

Nevertheless, it must be admitted that the Powers were in every case deliberately antagonistic to the claims of the defeated and that decisions reached were frequently the result of other considerations than that of satisfying nationalities—e.g., lands were transferred on the grounds that they were strategically important for the security of the new states (e.g., South Tyrol, peopled by Austrians, was handed to Italy).   The frontiers of the defeated states were not rectified, in the same way (e.g., the German minorities of Bohemia, once in the Austrian Empire, were still included in the new Slav state of Czecho-Slovakia).

The most obvious instances of injustice are :

(a) In the Defeated States

(i) Germans in Danzig and Memel were detached from their mother country.   The claims of Poland were preferred to those of Germany in the creation of the Polish Corridor to the sea and in the division of the Silesian industrial area.   Moreover, many Germans lived in the frontier provinces of Alsace-Lorraine, Holstein, and Bohemia, and these were also lost to Germany.

(ii) Austrians in the Tyrol, Galicia, and Bohemia were left under alien rule. Furthermore, it was expressly forbidden that Germany and Austria should unite.

(iii) The frontiers of post-War Hungary were restricted to the central part of the Hungarian Plain, leaving many Magyar peoples in Roumania, Czecho-Slovakia, and Yugo-Slavia.   (See Map 35.)

(b) In the New States

Large numbers of Ukrainians, a people of South Russia, were included in Poland and Roumania.   The boundaries of Poland were extended to include Lithuanian and Russian minorities, while Bulgarians and Serbs lived unhappily under Greek rule, and Yugo-Slavians along the Adriatic were subject to Italy.

71

MAP 34

PLEBISCITES

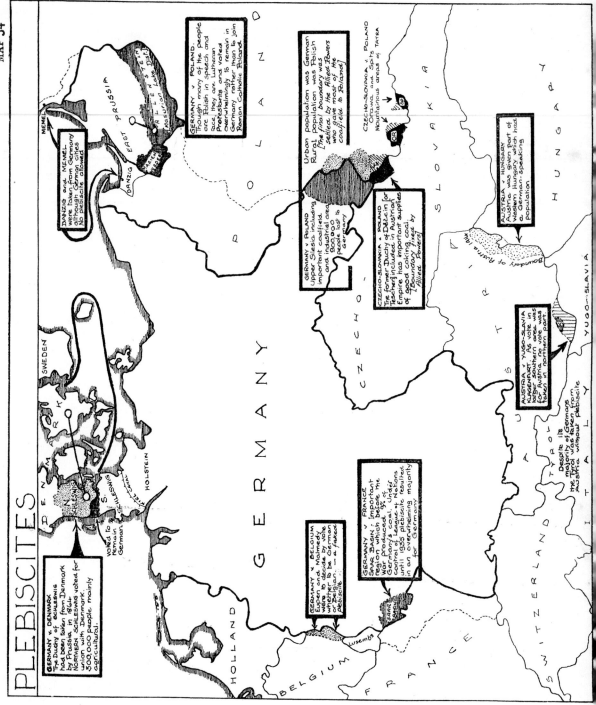

GERMANY v. DENMARK. The Duchy of SCHLESWIG had been taken from Denmark by Prussia in 1864. NORTHERN SCHLESWIG voted for union with Denmark. 500,000 people mainly agricultural.

voted to remain German. SCHLESWIG

DANZIG and MEMEL were taken from Germany although German cities. No plebiscite allowed.

GERMANY v POLAND. Though many of the people are Polish in speech and race, they are Lutheran Protestants and voted overwhelmingly to remain in Germany rather than to join Roman Catholic Poland.

Urban population was German Rural population was Polish [The final boundary was settled by the Allied Powers who gave most of the coalfield to Poland]

GERMANY v POLAND Upper Silesia including important coalfield and industrial area. 900,000 people lost to Germany

CZECHO-SLOVAKIA v POLAND The former Duchy of Delcin (or Teschen) included in Austrian Empire has important supplies of good coking coal. Region was divided by Allied Powers]

CZECHO-SLOVAKIA v POLAND Orrawa and Spits Mountainous areas of TATRA

AUSTRIA v HUNGARY Austria was given part of Western Hungary which had a German-speaking population

Boundary of Austria 1914

AUSTRIA v YUGO-SLAVIA KLAGENFURT. As vote in larger southern area was for Austria, no vote was taken in northern part.

Despite its majority of Germans the TYROL was taken from Austria without plebiscite

GERMANY v FRANCE SAAR BASIN. Important coal-producing region which before the War produced 8% of Germany's coal. Under control of League of Nations until 1935 plebiscite resulted in an overwhelming majority for Germany

GERMANY v BELGIUM Eupen and Malmedy were to decide by vote whether to be German or part of Belgium — a faked plebiscite.

HOLLAND

BELGIUM

Luxemb

FRANCE

DENMARK

SWEDEN

HOLSTEIN

THE CANAL

GERMANY

CZECHO-

SLOVAKIA

POLAND

EAST PRUSSIA

MASURIAN LAKE DIST

MEMEL

DANZIG

HUNGARY

AUSTRIA

TYROL

SWITZERLAND

ITALY

YUGO-SLAVIA

PLEBISCITES AND MINORITIES

Attempts were made to solve difficult problems of satisfying nationalities.

(a) *Plebiscites* were taken where there was a doubt to which state territory should be transferred. This was generally arranged where the victor states were likely to gain.

(b) *An interchange of nationals* from one state to another was arranged—*e.g.*, Turks were transferred from Greek territory and Greeks from Asia Minor to Greece.

(c) *Minority treaties*

Certain states made treaties with the League of Nations pledging their Governments to treat alien populations fairly and to respect their rights. The League undertook the responsibility of supervising the care of such Governments towards their subjects.

Map 34 illustrates (i) those boundaries which were adjusted on the decision of the Allied statesmen, (ii) the principal areas where plebiscites were arranged.

When the elections took place the voting was often influenced by propaganda; free voting was often impossible, for pressure was brought to bear upon the workers in the factories and the mines.

I. THE PLEBISCITE IN UPPER SILESIA

This important industrial area was originally Polish territory. It had been conquered by the Austrians and finally seized by Prussia in the eighteenth century. The Poles were in the majority in the countryside, but the Germans had developed the industrial resources and were more numerous in the towns. The plebiscite resulted in a German majority, but a large percentage (40 per cent.) voted for annexation with Poland. The question was therefore referred to the League of Nations, and a decision to partition the territory was made. Poland was granted only a third of the area, but this included mineral resources second only in importance to the Ruhr District. It should be noted that the Silesian coalfield is a natural unit and that, as a result of the plebiscite, it was divided by an international frontier and its economic life disturbed.

II. THE SAAR PLEBISCITE

This area was important for its coal-supplies, especially as they lay conveniently near the iron deposits ceded to France in Lorraine. France wanted this territory despite its almost wholly German population. By the Treaty of Versailles the Saar was to be administered by the League of Nations for fifteen years, at the end of which period a plebiscite was to determine the future destiny of the inhabitants. The voting took place in 1935, and there was an overwhelming majority in favour of Germany.

III. MINORITIES

The chief rights demanded for minorities were equal treatment before the law— the same civil and political rights as the majority, religious toleration, free use of their own tongue, including a free press and separate schools. As the League had no power to compel states to carry out its promises, the treaties have not served to improve the lot of many of the minority groups.

MAP 35

BREAK UP OF AUSTRIAN EMPIRE

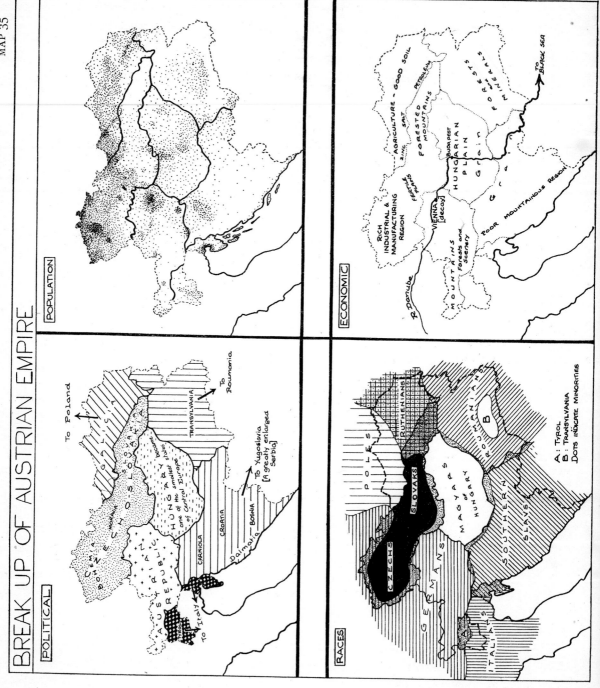

POPULATION

ECONOMIC

RICH INDUSTRIAL & MANUFACTURING REGION

AGRICULTURE – GOOD SOIL

SALT

ZINC

FERTILE PLAINS

PETROLEUM

FORESTED MOUNTAINS

VIENNA [decoy]

BUDAPEST

HUNGARIAN PLAIN

Grain

FORESTS

MINERALS

TO BLACK SEA

M O U N T A I N S

Forests and Scenery

POOR MOUNTAINOUS REGION

R. DANUBE

POLITICAL

To Poland

G A L I C I A

MORAVIA

B O H E M I A

C Z E C H O - S L O V A K I A

became one of the smallest states

A U S T R I A N   R E P U B L I C

H U N G A R Y
one of the smaller states of Central Europe

TRANSYLVANIA

To Roumania

CARNIOLA

CROATIA

Dalmatia – BOSNIA

To Yugoslavia
[A greatly enlarged Serbia]

To Italy

RACES

POLES

RUTHENIANS

GERMANS

CZECHS

SLOVAKS

MAGYARS of HUNGARY

R O U M A N I A N S

B

S O U T H E R N   S L A V S

ITALIANS

A

A : TYROL
B : TRANSYLVANIA
DOTS INDICATE MINORITIES

BREAK-UP OF THE AUSTRIAN EMPIRE

The most spectacular change in the post-War map of Europe was the disappearance of the Empire of Austria-Hungary. For a century it had been saved from collapse only by the will of its rulers, the Hapsburgs. There was no national unity in this Empire, Czechs, Poles, Croats, Slovenes being dominated by German and Magyar masters; yet because one dynasty linked together a huge territory in Central Europe, centring on the Middle Basin of the Danube, certain economic advantages accrued to its million inhabitants. There was free trade within the vast empire; a unified railway and river transport system and an outlet to the Adriatic Sea assisted the national trade and commerce.

This ramshackle empire could not withstand the strain of four years of war. On November 4 an armistice was concluded; a week later the Hapsburg Empire had ceased to exist. Its former territories were split into seven divisions, Austria and Hungary being reduced to the status of minor states.

Map 35 illustrates the areas, races, population, and economic resources of the partitioned empire. A comparative study of the four sketch-maps reveals the different characteristics of these divisions.

I. CZECHO-SLOVAKIA

Industrially and politically this was the most important of the new states of the old Austrian Empire. It consists of (*a*) *Bohemia*, a rich industrial and manufacturing region, with a fertile and intensively cultivated soil, densely populated with an intelligent Slavonic people, the Czechs, (*b*) *Moravia*, another important area, with a strategic position between the plains of the Vistula and the Danube, and (*c*) the mountainous area in the Carpathians, known as *Slovakia*, where the cultivable areas are few and the minerals unimportant. The population in this division is scanty and illiterate; communications are difficult.

Czecho-Slovakia thus inherited from the Austrian Empire industrial wealth and fertile land which enabled her to be self-supporting. She needed only peace to develop her resources.

Difficulties of Czecho-Slovakia

(i) Large numbers of minorities along the frontiers—Germans, Magyars, and Ruthenians—created internal difficulties of administration and led to unfriendly relations with Germany and Hungary.

(ii) The advantages which accrue from her central position in Europe are counter-balanced by the disadvantage of being surrounded by unfriendly neighbours.

II. HUNGARY

The Magyars of Hungary had settled in the plain of the Middle Danube, a vast grain-producing region. By conquest they had extended their authority over the Slav people in the surrounding mountain belt; there was a complementary exchange of the products of the plain and the mountains—grain for timber and minerals.

Difficulties of Hungary

The boundaries of the new state, however, had been drawn so as to exclude all but the purely Magyar-peopled areas of the plain, and the New Hungary soon found itself in the difficult position of having a surplus of wheat which it could market only in a world overstocked with grain. The collapse in world wheat-prices increased the difficulty in providing funds to buy the timber and other raw materials she required. Moreover, the capital, Buda-Pest, grew to its present size as the centre of a large kingdom which has since been reduced to a quarter of its former size.

Hungary is one of the most dissatisfied states of the new Europe; apart from her economic troubles there is the problem of unsatisfied nationalism, for over a third of the Magyar peoples live outside the boundaries of the country.

III. AUSTRIA

The new Austria comprised (*a*) a large area of the Eastern Alps, of little importance apart from its forests, alpine pastures, and scenic attractions, and (*b*) a small plain along the Danube surrounding Vienna.

Difficulties of Austria

(i) One-third of the population of Austria lives in the capital, Vienna. This was the old capital of the vast empire and one of the most important cities in Europe. It had thus attracted in pre-War days large numbers of officials engaged in government, banking, insurance, transport, and administration. These are no longer required, and Vienna does not any longer supply the needs of the people of a large empire—such as newspapers, clothes, and furniture. Moreover, the luxury-manufactures of the city are excluded from the new countries which surround Austria by high tariffs, and she cannot easily export goods to buy the food that her people cannot themselves grow.

(ii) Her population is entirely German in race and language, and it would seem natural that she should unite with Germany, but this was expressly forbidden by the Treaty of St Germain.[1]

IV. CROATIA, SLOVENIA, AND BOSNIA

These were the south-western provinces of the old Empire. They were largely mountainous areas of little economic importance. The people, however, were Slav in race and united with their kinsmen in Serbia to form the new Kingdom of the Serbs, Croats, and Slovenes, generally called Yugo-Slavia.

Difficulties of Yugo-Slavia

(i) It is a large country, but the economic resources are few and little developed.

(ii) The population includes large Magyar and German minorities, which complicate racial problems, already difficult enough to solve in a country peopled by Croat Roman Catholics and Serbian Orthodox believers. The Croats, who have had closer contact with the Germans, are more cultured than the Serbs and resent the greater influence of the Serbs.

V. TRANSYLVANIA

This includes (*a*) the western slopes of the Carpathians, rich in minerals and

---

[1] On March 12, 1938, the Germans marched into Austria and announced its inclusion in the German Reich.

developed industries, and (b) portions of the Hungarian plain, with pastures and grain-growing lands.   These gains doubled the size of the Kingdom of Roumania.

Difficulties of Roumania

(i) The minorities in Transylvania are Magyar and German.   These more cultured alien communities add to the difficulties of controlling a country already burdened with minority problems in the South—Bulgars in the Dobrudja and Ruthenians in Bessarabia.

(ii) The large estates of the nobility have been divided among the peasants, but the system of cultivation remains unprogressive; the peasants are poor and have difficulty in selling their grain in a world-market where prices are dictated by the costs of production in more advanced countries.

VI. GALICIA

This important province passed to Poland.   It is a wealthy area across the Carpathians.   Its soil is fertile and productive, while there are also coal, iron, zinc, salt, and petroleum resources.   The western part of the region is inhabited by Poles, but in the eastern portion the people are Ruthenians and have created a difficult minorities problem.   The attempts made by these people to unite with their kinsmen of the Ukraine S.S.R. have been frustrated by the Polish Government, and an insurrection was ruthlessly crushed.

VII. SOUTH TYROL : TRENTINO

Both these territories are Alpine districts.   In the Trentino the majority of the people are Italian.   In the Tyrol, however, the Germans are in the majority, and the union of both provinces to Italy created grave dissatisfaction.   (See Map 41 and notes.)

The satisfaction of the national aspirations of the various peoples included in the old Austrian Empire has created economic problems which affect the prosperity of all the states.   Each has tried to be self-supporting and has erected tariff-barriers against the rest.   Though they realize the folly of these restrictions on trade, attempts to form a Danubian Federation have proved so far unsuccessful.

THE MANDATE SYSTEM

During the War the Turkish provinces and the German colonies had been conquered by one or other of the Allied Powers, and the victors expected to retain their spoils just as conquerors in former wars had done.   The peace-makers in 1919, however, were bound by President Wilson's promises :

(a) " To make a free and impartial adjustment of colonial claims."

(b) To concern themselves with the interests of the people as well as the claims of the victors.

In the Covenant of the League it was laid down that the development of the backward nations should be regarded as a sacred trust by the more advanced nations. When the two enemy empires were partitioned the territory was not annexed but was held in trust by certain powers on behalf of the League of Nations.   The land was held

MANDATES

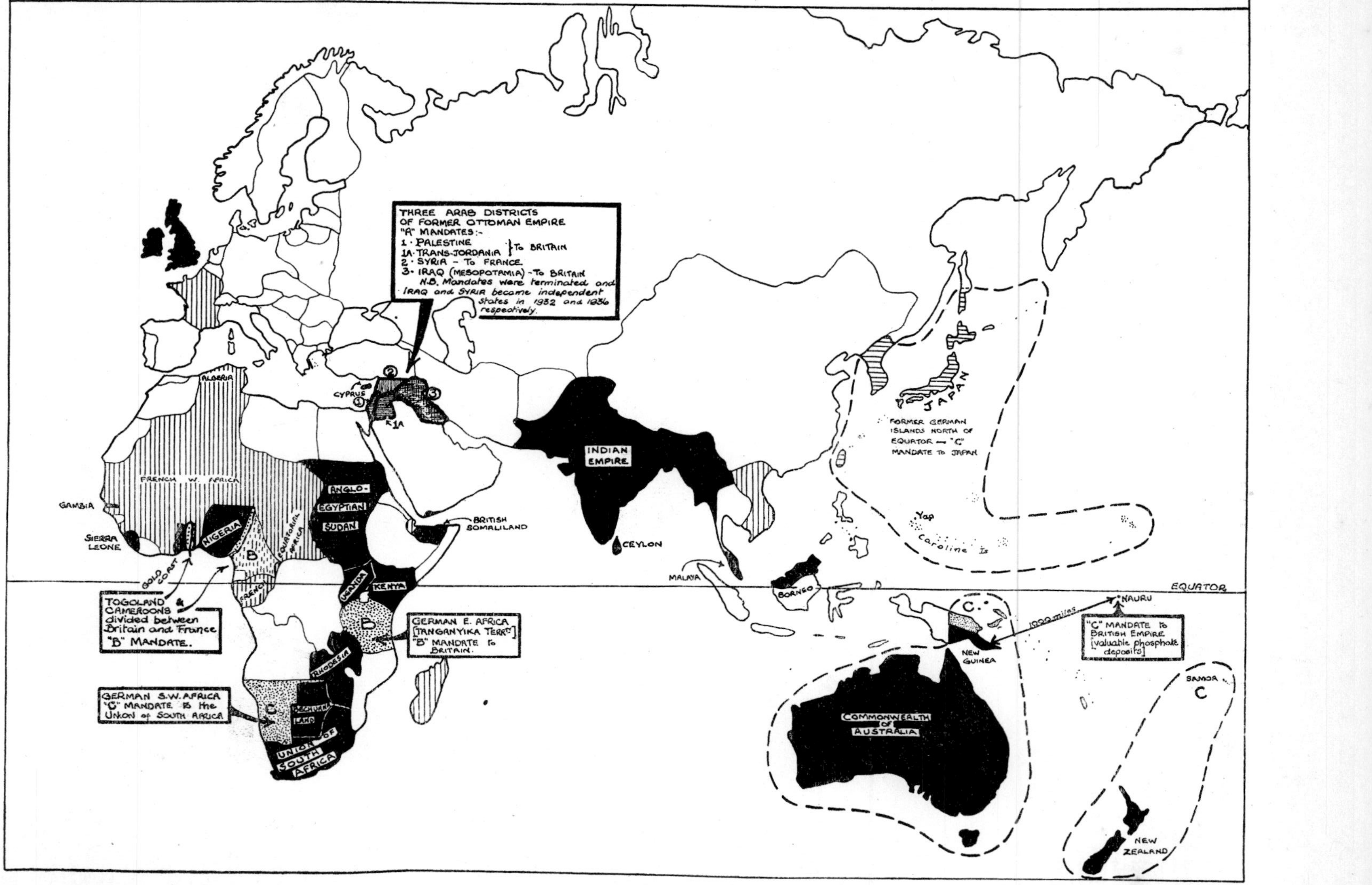
THREE ARAB DISTRICTS
OF FORMER OTTOMAN EMPIRE
"A" MANDATES:-
1. PALESTINE
1A. TRANS-JORDANIA } To BRITAIN
2. SYRIA - To FRANCE.
3. IRAQ (MESOPOTAMIA) - To BRITAIN
N.B. Mandates were terminated and IRAQ and SYRIA became independent states in 1932 and 1936 respectively.
CYPRUS
ALGERIA
FRENCH W. AFRICA
GAMBIA
SIERRA LEONE
GOLD COAST
NIGERIA
B
EQUATORIAL AFRICA
ANGLO-EGYPTIAN SUDAN
BRITISH SOMALILAND
UGANDA
KENYA
TOGOLAND & CAMEROONS divided between Britain and France "B" MANDATE.
GERMAN E. AFRICA [TANGANYIKA TERR.] "B" MANDATE to BRITAIN.
RHODESIA
BECHUANALAND
UNION OF SOUTH AFRICA
GERMAN S.W. AFRICA "C" MANDATE is the UNION of SOUTH AFRICA
INDIAN EMPIRE
CEYLON
MALAYA
BORNEO
JAPAN
FORMER GERMAN ISLANDS NORTH OF EQUATOR — "C" MANDATE To JAPAN
Yap
Caroline Is
EQUATOR
NAURU
1000 miles
"C" MANDATE to BRITISH EMPIRE [valuable phosphate deposits]
C.
NEW GUINEA
COMMONWEALTH of AUSTRALIA
SAMOA
C
NEW ZEALAND

'in mandate,' and the powers were known as 'mandataries,' the word 'mandate' implying a legal right granted by a superior authority. The mandataries accepted the responsibility of governing the territories, and they agreed to give an account of their stewardship in an annual report to the League of Nations.

I. THREE TYPES OF MANDATES

There were three different kinds of authority granted :

'A' Mandates. These were granted in respect of former Turkish territory in which the people were almost ready for self-government. (See Map 44 and notes on pp. 102, 103.)

'B' Mandates. These concerned territory, chiefly in Africa, where the people were in a backward state of civilization and could not govern themselves. The mandatory powers agreed to prohibit abuses such as the slave-trade, native exploitation, traffic in arms and drink. The territories were not to become fortified bases, and the natives could only be trained as soldiers for home defence. All other members of the League were to have equal rights in trade and commerce.

'C' Mandates. These were granted in respect of isolated territories, such as the Pacific Islands, or very undeveloped territory, such as the former German South-west Africa, where it seemed desirable that the mandatory power should assume fuller control governing the lands as part of their own territory.

II. DISTRIBUTION OF MANDATES

The U.S.A. refused to accept any mandates. It was left, therefore, to Britain and France to share the bulk of the work. Japan was satisfied with the former German islands in the Pacific.

(a) The British mandate in Tanganyika (East Africa) completed an 'all-red' route from the Cape to Cairo.

(b) The British mandate in Palestine afforded a further control over the Suez route to the East.

(c) Iraq became an independent state and a member of the League of Nations in 1932.

POLAND

In the eighteenth century Poland had fallen a prey to her aggressive neighbours —Russia, Austria, and Prussia—who partitioned the land among them. But the Poles held fast to their language and culture despite oppression, and they struggled for independence and unity.

I. DURING THE WAR

Polish leaders realized that the War provided an opportunity for gaining freedom, though at first they did not anticipate complete independence and struggled only for self-government. Though the mass of the Poles fought in the armies of Russia, an influential group, led by Pilsudski, supported Austria. In 1916 Russian Poland was overrun by the armies of the Central Powers ; the Germans occupied Warsaw and granted a measure of independence which did not come up to the expectation of the

MAP 37

POLAND

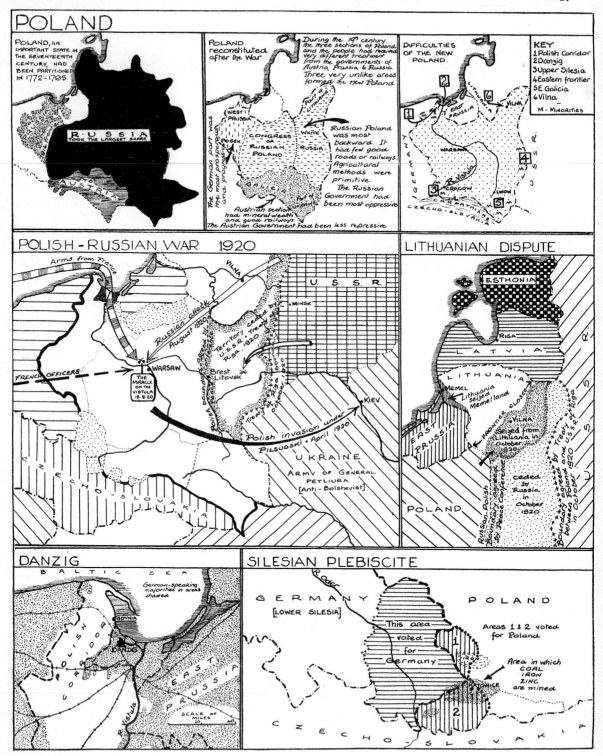

POLAND, AN IMPORTANT STATE IN THE SEVENTEENTH CENTURY, HAD BEEN PARTITIONED IN 1772-1795.

R·U·S·S·I·A TOOK THE LARGEST SHARE

AUSTRIA

POLAND reconstituted after the War

WEST PRUSSIA

POSEN

CONGRESS or RUSSIAN POLAND

GALICIA

Part of Lithuania

WHITE RUSSIA

The German part was the most prosperous and progressive

Austrian section had mineral wealth and good railways

The Austrian Government had been less repressive

During the 19th century the three sections of Poland and the people had received very different treatment from the governments of Austria, Prussia, & Russia. Three very unlike areas formed the new Poland.

Russian Poland was most backward. It had few good roads or railways Agricultural methods were primitive.

The Russian Government had been most oppressive

DIFFICULTIES OF THE NEW POLAND.

EAST PRUSSIA

VILNA

WARSAW

R. Vistula

CRACOW

LWOW

CARPATHIANS

CZECHO-SLOVAKIA

GERMANY

U.S.S.R.

M

KEY
1 Polish Corridor
2 Danzig
3 Upper Silesia
4 Eastern frontier
5 S.E. Galicia
6 Vilna
M – Minorities

POLISH-RUSSIAN WAR 1920

Arms from France

VILNA

Russian check August 1920.

U.S.S.R.

MINSK

Territory ceded by U.S.S.R. Treaty Riga 1920

Polish boundary

FRENCH OFFICERS

WARSAW

THE MIRACLE ON THE VISTULA 18·8·20

Brest Litovsk

Treaty of Riga

KIEV

Polish invasion under Pilsudski · April 1920

CZECHO-SLOVAKIA

UKRAINE

ARMY OF GENERAL PETLIURA [Anti-Bolshevist]

LITHUANIAN DISPUTE

ESTHONIA

RIGA

LATVIA

L I T H U A N I A

MEMEL

Lithuania seized Memelland

EAST PRUSSIA

FRONTIER CLOSED

VILNA seized from Lithuania in October 1920

POLAND

Russian-Polish Boundary agreed by Peace Conference

Ceded by Russia in October 1920

Boundary agreed by Treaty between Poland U.S.S.R. at Riga in October 1920

U.S.S.R.

DANZIG

B A L T I C   S E A

German-speaking majorities in areas shaded

GDYNIA

DANZIG

P O L I S H   C O R R I D O R

EAST PRUSSIA

R. Vistula

SCALE OF MILES

SILESIAN PLEBISCITE

R. Oder

G E R M A N Y [LOWER SILESIA]

P O L A N D

This area voted for Germany

Areas 1 & 2 voted for Poland

Area in which COAL IRON ZINC are mined

KATOWICE

1

2

C Z E C H O - S L O V A K I A

Poles.   In 1917 the Revolutionary Government of Russia endeavoured to obtain Polish support against Germany by a more generous offer of self-government.

In 1918 a group of Poles organized a National Committee in Paris and raised an army which fought on the Western Front.   The Allies in return promised the Poles complete independence.   The independent Polish State was proclaimed at Warsaw and in Galicia immediately after the collapse of the Central Powers.

II. PEACE CONFERENCE

The new state was represented at the Peace Conference, and its independence was recognized.   The western frontier was agreed upon—the provinces of Posen, West Prussia, and Galicia were to be included in the new Poland.   The eastern frontier was settled provisionally.   *N.B.*—Poland was generously treated at the Peace Conference. She had the strong support of President Wilson ;   France regarded a strong Poland as a useful bulwark against German and Russian aggression.   (See Map 31.)

III. FRONTIER PROBLEMS AFTER THE PEACE

(a) *Eastern Frontier with Bolshevist Russia*

The disturbed state of Russia after the War (see Maps 27 and 28) offered the Poles an opportunity to secure a more favourable eastern frontier.   Pilsudski's armies over-ran the Ukraine and occupied Kiev in April, 1920.   When the Russians began a counter-offensive which brought the Bolshevist armies to the outskirts of Warsaw, the very existence of Poland was threatened.   With the aid of the French the Russian army was driven back, and in 1920 a treaty was signed at Riga by which Poland secured the more favourable frontiers shown on the map.   (The boundary was changed slightly at a second treaty made in March, 1921.)

(b) *Dispute with Lithuania*

The new state of Lithuania claimed Vilna as its capital ;   Poland wanted the city on the grounds that it was an ancient centre of Polish culture.   The dispute was referred to the League of Nations, but before the League's decision could be enforced, an army of Poles, officially disowned by the Polish Government, took possession of the city in 1920.   Three years later the Polish claim was recognized by the League.

(c) *Eastern Galicia*

The attempt to form an independent state of Ukrainians in Eastern Galicia was crushed by Pilsudski in 1919.

(d) *Upper Silesia*

See Map 34 and notes on p. 73.

(e) *Polish Corridor*

President Wilson had promised that Poland should have access to the sea.   This involved adding to the indisputably Polish territory an area along the coast west of the Vistula delta in which there was a mixed population of Germans and Slavs.   Germany strongly objected, because East Prussia was cut off from the rest of the state ;   when the German President wished to visit his family estates in East Prussia he had to cross a foreign state.   Moreover, in spite of the fact that its population was overwhelmingly

F

German, the Poles claimed the city of Danzig as the 'natural outlet' of the basin of the Vistula. A compromise resulted in the creation of a tiny independent state—the 'Free City of Danzig'—under the supervision of the League of Nations. Neither country is satisfied. Poland has constructed vast artificial harbours a few miles away from Danzig at Gdynia, and the new port threatens the prosperity of the old.

(f) Teschen (Czech: Děcin)

A division of the former Austrian territory of Teschen, an area with valuable coal-mines, was arranged by the Allied statesmen. There was considerable friction with Czecho-Slovakia; the final agreement gave the larger portion of the area to the Poles, but the coal-mines were granted to Czecho-Slovakia.

IV. DIFFICULTIES OF MODERN POLAND

(a) External

Poland is geographically part of the vast northern plain of Europe. Its nucleus is the basin of the River Vistula. The frontiers are artificial, with the exception of that to the south where the Carpathians separate Poland from Czecho-Slovakia. To the west lies Germany, and to the east, Russia, both potentially powerful states, which before the War shared most of Poland.

With both of these powerful neighbours there are likely sources of dispute:

> (i) *With Germany*
> The Polish Corridor and Danzig.
> Silesia.
> (ii) *With Russia*
> The indefinite eastern frontier.
> Ruthenian minorities in Eastern Galicia who wish to join with the Soviet Ukraine.

There are further frontier troubles:

> (iii) *With Lithuania*
> Vilna.
> (iv) *With Czecho-Slovakia*
> Teschen.

(b) Internal

The difficulties of the first few years after the War—the fear of Bolshevism, the general poverty of the country, which had no money, no army, no rolling-stock—proved too much for the inexperienced democratic Government. Poland, after 1926, was ruled by the military dictator, Pilsudski.

The poverty of the people, many of whom live on a diet of black bread and potatoes, remains acute. The pre-War emigration to the U.S.A. has practically stopped. The national minorities cause much unrest. More than 8 per cent. of the population are Jews, who live in the towns, a race apart, and under almost unbelievable conditions of squalor and poverty. Anti-Semitic agitation is growing and provides the Polish Government with one of its major problems.

SINCE THE PEACE SETTLEMENT

REPARATIONS : THE ECONOMIC CRISIS (1929–1932)

THE victorious Allied Powers were agreed that Germany should pay the cost of the War.[1] The French, in particular, desired compensation to cover the expense of rebuilding their war-stricken areas. The efforts to collect indemnities or reparations from defeated Germany lasted until 1932.

First Stage (1919–1923) : Fixing the sum due—the first default and the penalty—the occupation of the Ruhr Coalfield.

Second Stage (1924–1929) : The Dawes Plan.

Third Stage (1929–1932) : Financial crisis and the abandonment of reparations at the Treaty of Lausanne.

I. FIRST STAGE (1919–1923)

The Treaty of Versailles did not fix any definite total sum. The Allied Powers appointed a Reparations Committee to make out the bill and decide how and when the debtor should meet it—that is, how much should be paid in money and how much in deliveries of coal. Meanwhile a conference at Spa in July, 1920, allocated the sums which were to be extorted from Germany for the victorious Powers.

Not until April, 1921, did the Reparations Committee fix the total liability at 136,000,000,000 marks ; this was an impossibly high figure in view of the condition of Germany. The people were starving, and raw materials were scarce. Moreover, the Treaty of Versailles had taken away 15 per cent. of the productive resources of the country (territory, mercantile marine, etc. ; see Map 32 and notes on pp. 67, 68).

Under the threat of invasion the German Government accepted the liability, and an attempt was made to pay the first instalment by deliveries of coal and the sale of securities held by German investors in foreign countries. In December, 1922, the amounts promised had not been paid ; President Poincaré decided to act, and despite British protests, a French-Belgian army entered the Ruhr Coalfield—the principal manufacturing area of Germany. The Germans attempted ' passive resistance ' ; the miners refused to go down the coal-mines, and the factory-hands went on strike.

Results of the Invasion of the Ruhr

(*a*) The economic ruin of Germany was complete. German industry and trade were brought to a standstill.

(*b*) The German currency collapsed.

	Marks to the £	
1914	20	
1919	250	Terms of Treaty of Versailles announced.
April, 1921	500	Amount of reparations fixed.
November, 1921	1,000	Silesian award ; see p. 73.
1922	35,000	Eve of occupation of Ruhr.
End of 1923	16,000,000,000,000	

---

[1] The slogans at the 1918 election in Great Britain were "Hang the Kaiser" and "Make Germany Pay."

The results of this depreciation of the mark were :

(i) A boom in trade and employment, for the cost of goods in marks was so small that they undersold all competitors in the markets of the world.

(ii) The middle classes in Germany—especially those with incomes fixed in marks from interest on loans, mortgages, rents—were ruined. A man who had on deposit at the bank his life-savings of, say, 20,000 marks (*i.e.*, £1000) found that they were worth the price of a post-card stamp. The middle classes were thus reduced to the level of the poorest working class. It was from this class that the first National Socialists were drawn. (See pp. 96-98.)

(iii) The aristocracy, holding most of their wealth in land, were not so greatly affected, while industrial magnates who could borrow money at the beginning of a month and pay back the same *nominal* amount at the end of the month, made vast fortunes.

(c) The voluntary payment of reparations and the deliveries of coal ceased. The French failed to recover sufficient even to pay the cost of the occupation.

(d) The wartime feeling of English people against Germany was replaced by a more sympathetic understanding. The British Government disapproved of the French action, and the relations between the former allies were strained.

MAP 38

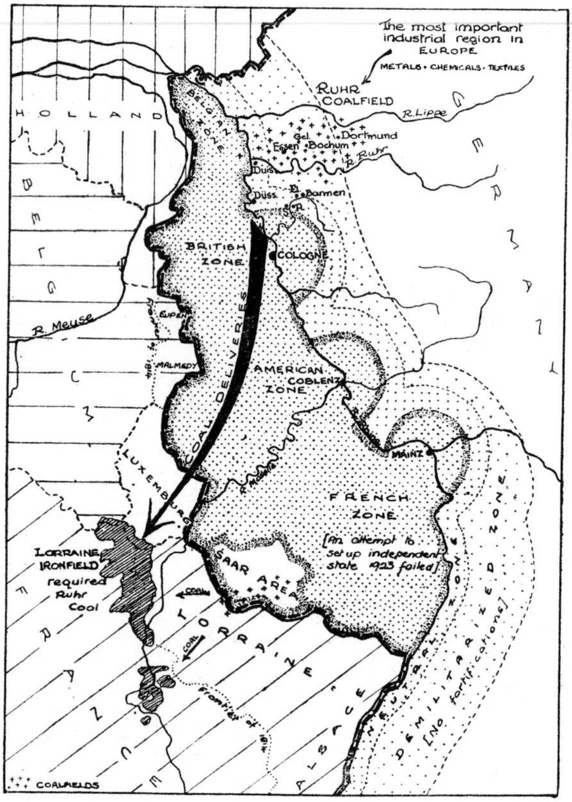

OCCUPATION OF THE RUHR

The German frontier is shown by a thick line. The area closely stippled was occupied by Allied troops after the Armistice. The demilitarized zone was the area in which Germany was forbidden to erect fortresses or maintain an army. On March 8, 1921, Marshal Foch occupied the Rhine ports of Dusseldorf and Duisberg-Ruhrort. On January 11 French and Belgian troops entered the Ruhr Coalfield.

II. SECOND STAGE (1924–1929)

The Dawes Plan

In September, 1923, in view of the impending ruin of the whole of Germany, the new German ministry of Stresemann called off the 'passive resistance' in the Ruhr, while early in the following year the ministry of Poincaré, which had been responsible for the short-sighted French policy, was replaced by the Radical Government of Herriot.

A committee of experts, under the chairmanship of an American, General Dawes, produced a plan which arranged for more limited annual reparation payments and the reorganization of German currency. (1 Reichsmark—1,000,000,000,000 old marks.) To provide financial resources to enable the German Government to carry on, an international loan was floated. The success of this loan led to further borrowings. Money poured into Germany, especially from the U.S.A., and with this borrowed money Germany was not only able to make reparations payments, but also could afford to re-equip her damaged railways and industrial plant and rebuild her cities.

At the beginning of 1929 a new committee, known after its American chairman as the Young Committee, amended the scheme of reparation payments. Germany's acceptance of the Young Plan was followed by the evacuation of the Rhineland Army of Occupation.

The five years, 1924–1929, were a welcome return to prosperity, peace, and progress, but the basis of the improvement was the continuance of American loans to Europe :

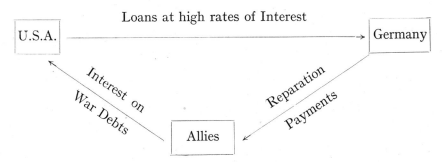

This position was unsound and unsafe ; during the War the Allies had obtained supplies of food and arms on a large scale from America. European countries emerged from the War impoverished and greatly in debt to American financiers. Yet instead of paying back their debt by sending manufactures, they were importing from America more than they were sending back ; thus they were increasing rather than reducing the debt. Prohibitive U.S.A. tariffs excluded foreign goods and thus made it difficult for Europe to pay what it owed.

III. THIRD STAGE (1929–1932)

The World Economic Crisis

During 1929 a speculation boom in the U.S.A. made it more profitable for Americans to lend their money at home than in Europe. American loans to Europe practically ceased, and so was precipitated the most devastating economic crisis in post-War history. It lasted until 1933.

(a) General Features of the Crisis

(i) A general fall in the prices of foodstuffs and raw materials, and consequently a restriction of production which led to much unemployment.

(ii) In order to protect their industries and agriculture, countries raised their tariffs and restricted imports in various ways ; thus international trade was almost brought to a standstill.

(iii) Debtor countries, *i.e.*, those in which foreigners had made investments, either defaulted in their payments of interest (*e.g.*, Chile) or threatened to default (*e.g.*, Germany), for to pay the interest they had to send goods ; but the produce they could have exported was not wanted, and its value had greatly decreased. It was impossible

85

to borrow more money from the U.S.A., for Americans were no longer ready to lend to foreigners threatened with bankruptcy.

(iv) Unable to pay interest by sending goods, debtor countries were forced to send to their creditors (*e.g.*, to U.S.A.) their remaining stock of gold or else to default. Thus the world's supplies of gold was passing to America.

(b) Effects of the Crisis in Germany

(i) Exports and imports fell sharply, and the number of unemployed rose to over 6,000,000.

(ii) The prevailing distress drove the Social-Democratic Party from power (March, 1930). The new Reichstag saw an increase in the Nazi representatives from 12 to 107. The new ministry ruled by Presidential Decree, and democratic government disappeared.

(iii) An attempt to arrange a *Zollverein* (Customs Union) with Austria was foiled by France.

(iv) The failure of the most important bank in Austria in May, 1931, caused a panic which spread across Europe. Germany threatened to default on her interest payments as well as in reparations.

(v) The President of the U.S.A. (Hoover), in June, 1931, suggested a moratorium for a year (*i.e.*, non-collection of international debts or reparations).

(vi) Before the moratorium expired, Germany announced its incapacity and unwillingness to pay any further reparations. A conference called at Lausanne in June, 1932, agreed to cancel them in exchange for bonds to the value of £150,000,000.

(c) Effects in Great Britain

(i) The slump in world prices had disorganized British trade. Foreigners could not afford to buy British manufactures ; unemployment increased, and the Government was unable to balance its budget owing to a fall in the receipts from income tax.

(ii) Foreign financiers who had money on loan in London withdrew their balances at a time when British financiers were unable to collect the money which had been lent to Germans, and when foreign railways and Governments were defaulting in their payments of interest to British investors.

(iii) The Bank of England was drained of most of its gold reserve, and in September, 1931, the newly formed National Government had to come off the ' gold standard.' The £ sterling depreciated by about 25 per cent. This fall from the gold standard was followed a year later by a default in the payment of instalments on the American debt. The conference at Lausanne in 1932 had cancelled the other inter-allied debts.

(iv) The collapse of the Labour Government. See p. 114.

(d) Position of the U.S.A.

Before the War the U.S.A. was a ' debtor ' country. Its exports greatly exceeded its imports, and the difference represented the payment of interest on European investments in America.

During the War enormous quantities of food and materials were bought in the U.S.A., and Europe was too busy fighting to be able to send goods in return. America emerged from the War no longer a ' debtor ' country, but the principal ' creditor ' country in the world.

Since the War the Americans have endeavoured to continue their pre-War policy of sending vast exports to Europe and at the same time have restricted imports by a prohibitively high tariff; but this method will no longer work, for European countries are now the 'debtors' and have to send to America not only goods in payment of goods bought from America, but also additional goods representing interest on, or repayment of, their debts. The Americans wished to sell their goods in Europe but did not allow Europe to pay for them! Even when they were paid for in gold—and most of the precious metal has been remitted to the U.S.A.—the gold was not really wanted and had to be 'sterilized'—*i.e.*, buried away in the mountains of Kentucky! Yet the excess of U.S.A exports over imports continues; it means that the world is becoming more and more in debt to America, which, unlike most creditors, does its utmost to stop repayment.

THE LITTLE ENTENTE

The reconstruction of Central Europe at the Peace Conference brought into existence new states mutually suspicious and aggressive, conditions equally ruinous to their development and dangerous to the stability of Europe.

The drawing together of the three states, Czecho-Slovakia, Yugo-Slavia, and Roumania, into an alliance known as the Little Entente was therefore an important political development, for the economic activity of this Danubian area was doomed to extinction if these newly formed states remained permanently divided.

Two important factors brought about the formation of the alliance:
(*a*) The active opposition of Hungary to the Peace Settlement.
(*b*) The fear, common to all three states, that Hungary would resist it.

The Magyars of Hungary had been unjustly treated. Large groups were under the rule of their former subjects. Hungary's irredentist aspirations threatened the security of Czecho-Slovakia, Yugo-Slavia, and Roumania. Co-operation to frustrate the dangerous activities of Hungary was essential. In 1919 they united to attack Hungary.

Czecho-Slovakian statesmen were chiefly responsible for building up the alliance, and the initiative came from them because the needs of Czecho-Slovakia were great. It was an inland state with long frontiers not easily defended, and dependent therefore for its security and prosperity on the friendliness of its neighbours. The statesmen had no easy task in overcoming the mutual distrust of the three states.

The internal weakness of each state strengthened the necessity for union against the common foe. Internal problems were similar in all three states; each Government had to deal with groups of minorities, and they were faced with the task of reorganizing their agriculture and industries and building up their foreign trade. (See note on p. 75.) Each Government met with difficulties in its attempt to organize an internal administration on democratic lines.

I. STEPS IN THE FORMATION OF THE LITTLE ENTENTE

Three treaties were concluded: in 1920, between Czecho-Slovakia and Yugo-Slavia, and in 1921, between Yugo-Slavia and Roumania, and between Czecho-Slovakia and Roumania. In 1933 the alliance was strengthened, and a permanent council of ministers to direct a common foreign policy was established.

MAP 39

LITTLE ENTENTE

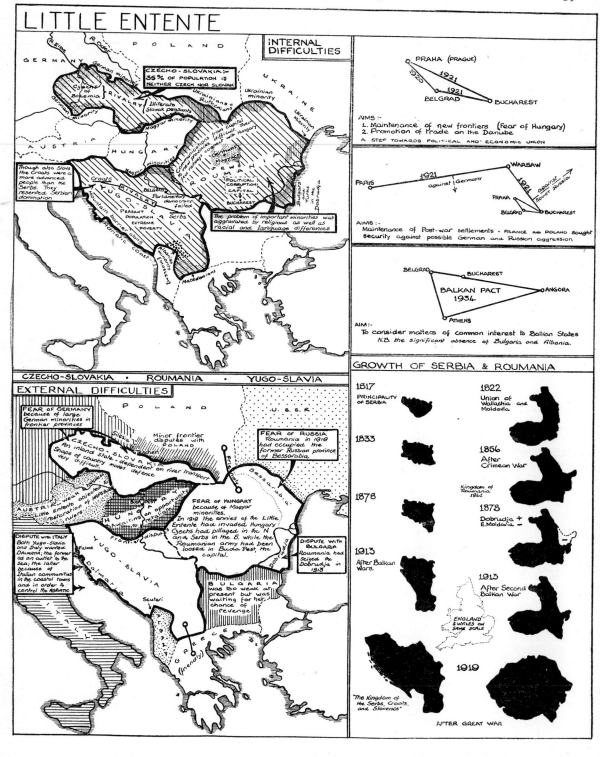

The Little Entente Powers, thus united, were able to exert more influence in international affairs—*e.g.*, they had a common policy at Geneva.

II. FOREIGN RELATIONS OF THE LITTLE ENTENTE POWERS

The three countries had been encouraged to come to an understanding by France, who saw in the alliance and its adherence to the Peace Treaties a strong guarantee of support against possible German or Hungarian aggression. She supplied them with arms and money. Alliances concluded in 1921, on the one hand between *Poland* and *Roumania*, providing for mutual assistance if attacked by Russia, and on the other hand between France and Poland, promising mutual support, completed the grouping of the Powers of Central Europe and France.

THE BALKAN PACT

Before the War the Great Powers exploited the jealousies which existed among the Balkan States to extend their own influence. From about 1929 a movement towards co-operation began between Yugo-Slavia, Greece, Roumania, and their former enemy, Turkey.

The object was to settle their own differences, so that the Powers would have no excuse for intervening.

Difficulties which had to be overcome

(a) The Animosity of the Balkan States towards Turkey

During the nineteenth century the Balkan States had shaken off the oppressive rule of the Turks, but it was not until after the War that they began to realize that the New Turkey had no desire to threaten their security. In 1930 Greece and Turkey came to an agreement by which they promised to respect their common frontier. This was an important step towards the formation of the Pact of 1934.

(b) The Mutual Jealousies of the Balkan Powers

The Balkan States had never been united except in their common opposition to Turkey. The territorial changes after the second Balkan War (1912) had left irreconcilable bitterness (see Map 4) between Bulgaria and her neighbours, and the new settlement at Neuilly accentuated it. She was not prepared to join any pact to guarantee frontiers with which she was completely dissatisfied.

(c) The rivalry between Italy and Yugo-Slavia

Italian influence in Albania, which alienated Yugo-Slavia, also prevented Italy from joining any Balkan alliance.

Greek statesmen persistently advocated the alliance, which was concluded in Athens in 1934.

THE DECLINE OF DEMOCRACY

I. THE TRIUMPH OF DEMOCRACY IN EUROPE

Throughout the nineteenth century the Liberals of Europe had striven to obtain constitutions based on parliamentary government, political freedom, and equality; by 1914 they had achieved their aims except in Germany, Austria, and Russia.

MAP 40

THE DECLINE OF DEMOCRACY

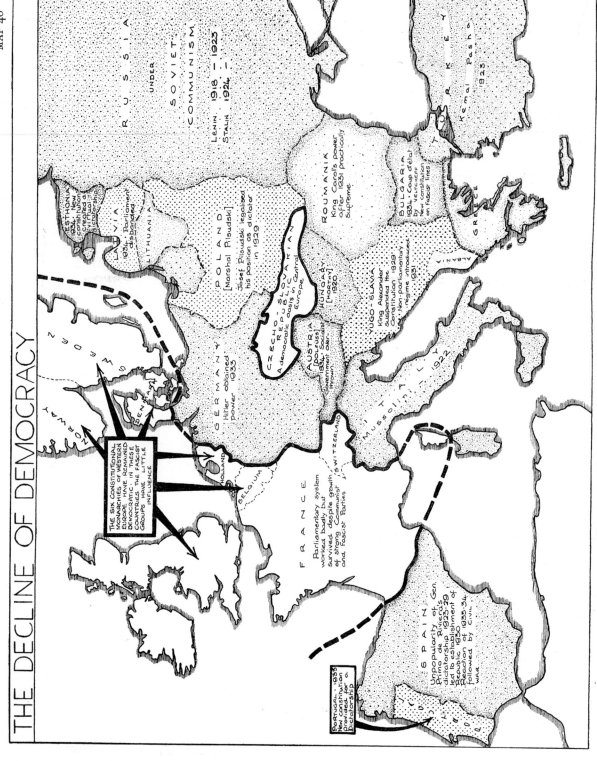

R U S S I A

UNDER

SOVIET

COMMUNISM

Lenin 1918 - 1923
Stalin 1924 -

ESTHONIA
1934. New
constitution
created a
virtual
dictatorship

LATVIA
1934. Parliament
disbanded

LITHUANIA

POLAND
[Marshal Pilsudski]
Josef Pilsudski legalised
his position as dictator
in 1929

CZECHO-SLOVAKIAN
REPUBLIC
A democratic oasis in Central
Europe.

ROUMANIA
King Carol's power
after 1931 practically
supreme.

BULGARIA
1934. Coup d'état
by vaer.cerer
New constitution
on Fascist lines

T U R K E Y
Kemal Pasha
1923

GREECE

GERMANY
Hitler obtained
power 1933

AUSTRIA
[Dolfuss]
1934. Socialist
Government over-
thrown.

HUNGARY
[Horthy]
1920

YUGO-SLAVIA
King Alexander
suspended the
Constitution 1929
Non-parliamentary
regime introduced
1931

ALBANIA

I T A L Y
Mussolini 1922

SWEDEN

NORWAY

DENMARK

THE SIX CONSTITUTIONAL
MONARCHIES OF WESTERN
EUROPE HAVE REMAINED
DEMOCRATIC. IN THESE
COUNTRIES THE FASCIST
GROUPS HAVE LITTLE
INFLUENCE.

HOLLAND

BELGIUM

F R A N C E
Parliamentary system
worked badly but
survived despite growth
of strong Communist
and Fascist Parties

SWITZERLAND

S P A I N
Unpopularity of Gen.
Primo de Rivera's
dictatorship 1923-29
led to establishment of
Republic 1930.
Reaction of 1933-34
followed by Civil
War.

PORTUGAL 1933
New constitution
provided for a
Dictatorship

The fall of the two great empires, Germany and Austria, and the disruption of Russia, the chief centres of autocratic rule, seemed a happy augury for the future of democratic government. After the War democratic government was established in the new states, whose rulers recognized the wisdom of adopting constitutions modelled on those of the Western Powers. In every European country, except Russia, where a new form of government—a Communist dictatorship—was maintained, the principle of representative government was accepted.

II. THE WEAKNESS OF THE NEW DEMOCRACIES

The statesmen of Europe after the War were faced with political and economic problems which they could not solve ; they had difficulty in maintaining law and order. In circumstances which called for strong rule and decisive action, they displayed fear and ineptitude ; they permitted opposition parties to raise private armies illegally and allowed the constitutions they had sworn to maintain to be openly and systematically undermined. The reasons for this failure of parliamentary government, which was most complete in those countries where experience in democratic rule was most limited, are :

(a) The citizens had not that political training which successful democratic government demands. The sudden transition from autocratic rule had given no opportunities to acquire such training in either local or national government.

(b) The parliamentary parties, representing conflicting class interests, minority and religious groups, were too opposed on fundamental questions to accept loyally the decisions of the majority. Instead of having, as in England, a Government Party and an Opposition Party ready to take office if the Government Party were defeated in the House of Commons, they were violent and irresponsible factions whose animosity intensified party strife. When such groups could not get their way constitutionally they were prepared to resort to any illegal methods which might prove effective.

(c) There were still many people in these states who did not accept the principle of democracy. Included in this group were the class of army officers, state officials of the old *régimes*, and many members of the middle classes whose positions had been materially worsened. These dissentient groups were only too ready to pour scorn on the ineffectiveness of the new Parliaments and to recall the glories of the past. Many of the Republican Governments failed to arouse any enthusiasm for the new democratic institutions, not realizing that the masses must be inspired by systematic propaganda.

III. INFLUENCE OF COMMUNIST RUSSIA—RISE OF FASCIST DICTATORSHIPS

Communist propaganda from the U.S.S.R. spread through Europe. To counteract its disruptive influence among the working classes, powerful groups of the dissatisfied middle class, frequently supported financially by wealthy manufacturers, created new political parties, which had the following characteristics :

(a) They glorified their own country and poured scorn on any international outlook of the Government.

(b) They prejudiced the people against certain classes of citizens, *e.g.*, Jews and Freemasons.

MAP 41

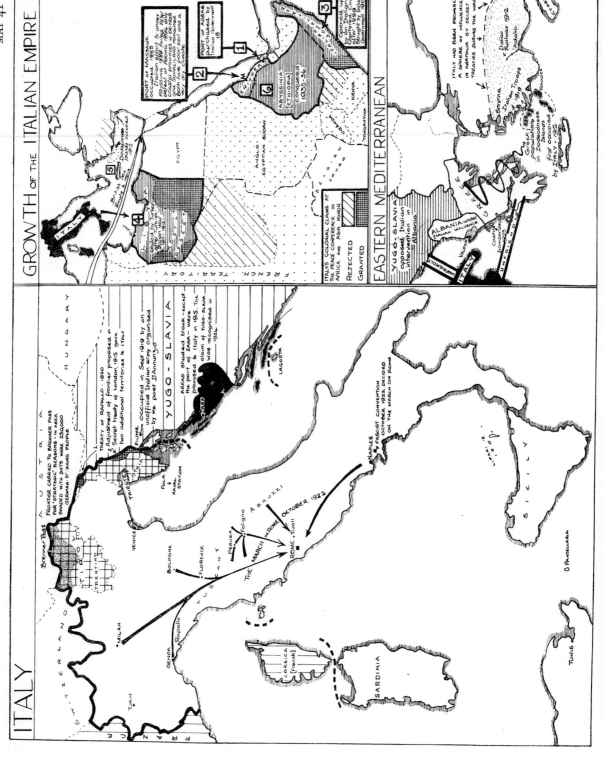

GROWTH of the ITALIAN EMPIRE

PORT of MASSAWA
occupied 1885
Italian effort to annex
Abyssinia suffered a
defeat at Adowa. Only
coastal provinces of ERITREA
became Italian. Both have poor soil and a
very dry climate.

PORT of ASSAB
Purchased by
Italian Government

Opened up
by the Italian
Government
after 1898.
Bought by Italian
Government 1882.

Dodecanese
islands occupied
1912

Ceded by Turkey
after the Turkish
War of 1911-1912

ABYSSINIA
(ETHIOPIA)
Conquered
1935-36

EGYPT

ANGLO
EGYPTIAN SUDAN

UGANDA

KENYA

TANGANYIKA

FRENCH TERRITORY

BRITISH SOM &
ITALIAN SOM &
SOM

ITALY'S COLONIAL CLAIMS AT
THE PEACE CONFERENCE IN
AFRICA AND ASIA MINOR

REJECTED
GRANTED

EASTERN MEDITERRANEAN

ITALY HAD BEEN PROMISED
A SPHERE OF INFLUENCE
IN ANATOLIA BY SECRET
TREATIES DURING THE WAR

Smyrna
Italian Troops
1919

K. Italian
Railway 1912
Adalia

Greek populations
in Dodecanese
islands first
occupied by
Italy 1912

Rhodes

YUGO-SLAVIA
opposed Italian
intervention in
Albania.

ALBANIA under
ITALIAN INFLUENCE

Valona

GREECE

ITALY

Corfu
bombarded

ITALY

SWITZERLAND

AUSTRIA

HUNGARY

Brenner Pass
Frontier carried to Brenner Pass
for 'strategic' reasons. In area
shaded with dots were 250,000
German-speaking people.

TYROL

TRENTINO

VENICE

TRIESTE

ISTRIA

POLA
Naval Station

FIUME

YUGO-SLAVIA

FRANCE

TURIN

MILAN

Rapallo

GENOA

BOLOGNA

TUSCANY

FLORENCE

PERUGIA

Foligno

THE MARCH on ROME OCTOBER 1922

ABRUZZI

ROME Tivoli

Naples

FASCIST CONVENTION
OCTOBER 1922 DECIDED
ON THE MARCH ON ROME.

CORSICA
(French)

SARDINIA

SICILY

TUNIS

O PANTELLARIA

LIPARI Is.

LAGOSTA

TREATY of RAPALLO. 1920
1. Frontier proposed in
Secret Treaty of London, 1915 gave
two additional territories to ITALY

2. Adjustment of frontier proposed in

AREAS shaded black except
the port of Zara - were
promised to Italy in 1915. The
claim of Yugo-Slavia
was recognised in
1924.

FIUME, occupied in Sept. 1919 by an
unofficial Italian army organised
by the poet D'Annunzio.

(c) They introduced uniforms and ceremonial to attract the attention of the indifferent masses.

(d) They resorted to violent methods whenever necessary to further their ends.

(e) They had no belief in the virtues of democracy, preferring to follow the lead of some forceful dictator.

It was in Italy, where Parliamentary institutions had never flourished, that such a leader first established himself. This was Benito Mussolini, who founded his Fascist Party in 1919. (See below.)

The map shows how similar parties flourished throughout Europe. The failure of the Parliamentary Governments to deal with the misery arising after the World Economic Crisis (1929–1932) strengthened the Fascist Parties. Dictators ruled in Germany, Austria, Poland, Yugo-Slavia, and Bulgaria; in other countries, such as Finland, Roumania, Greece, Portugal, and the smaller Baltic countries, the Parliament failed to control the Ministry. Even in France, Holland, and Belgium the growth of Fascism created difficulties for the Parliamentary leaders.

Only in England, Norway, and Sweden was the influence of the Fascist parties negligible. Czecho-Slovakia has maintained her position with difficulty, surrounded as she is by a *bloc* of Fascist neighbours.

For Germany, see Map 42 and notes on pp. 96–98.

ITALY

I. PRE-WAR PROBLEMS AND DIFFICULTIES

Italian unification was completed in 1870, but there remained four major problems:

(a) *Rivalry between Provincial States*

For centuries the provinces of Italy had been divided. After their union it was necessary for them to forget their former rivalry and jealousy and to sink their differences for the common good. This they were loath to do.

(b) *Poverty of the People*

Italy is not rich in mineral wealth, and much of the land is either infertile and uncultivable highland or malarial marsh. The dense population finds difficulty in supporting itself.

(c) *Quarrel between Church and State*

The Pope refused to recognize the Italian Government, because of its occupation of Rome (1870). The conflict between Church and State both weakened and harassed the Government.

(d) *Imperial Ambitions*

Seeking prestige and desirous of equality with the other Great Powers, Italy entered into the scramble for colonial territory. A late-comer, she gained little of value— mostly deserts in the north of Africa (see map).

II. EFFECTS OF THE GREAT WAR AND THE PEACE SETTLEMENT

Italy entered the War in 1915 only because she saw an opportunity of satisfying further ambitions.   She joined the Allies because they offered her more than the Central Powers, and she felt they would be able to fulfil their promises.

The Peace Settlement disappointed Italy.   The Allied offers (made in the Secret Treaty of London, 1915) were not fulfilled, as the promises made to the Italians were intended to be at the expense of Austria-Hungary.   The break-up of the Austrian Empire, however, left the territory claimed in the hands of another Ally—Serbia, now become Yugo-Slavia.

Hence Italy *received*
- the Trentino,
- South Tyrol,
- Istria and the district round Trieste,
- the ports of Zara and Lagosta ;

but she *failed to secure* what had been *promised*
- all the Dalmatian Coast
- a Protectorate over Albania
- part of the former German Empire in Africa.

her aim was to secure control of the Adriatic

She *did not even secure*
- the port of Fiume, which had a large Italian population. (*N.B.*—It was one of Yugo-Slavia's outlets to the sea.)

She was *unable to hold*
- part of Asia Minor (Adalia) which the New Turkey reconquered.

Bitterly disappointed, the people blamed the Government ; there was great discontent throughout the country.

Fiume Incident, 1919

The first manifestation of this dissatisfaction occurred in 1919, when a group of soldiers, led by D'Annunzio, attacked the city of Fiume.   The Italian Government was forced by the Allies to expel them.   They returned to Italy indignant and disgusted at the weakness of their Government.

III. RISE OF FASCISM

The general conditions which encouraged the growth of Fascism have been considered on pp. 89–93.

Post-War conditions in Italy were particularly difficult.   The economic problems grew more and more serious.   There were peasant risings in the south and industrial strikes in the cities of the north.   The Government seemed powerless to restrain the increasing violence.

In 1919 Mussolini formed an organization of ex-service men as a party of action which would bring about a " radical transformation of the Italian State."   His organization became the nucleus of the Fascist Party (*Fasces*—Roman rods which symbolized the authority of the Consul).

It gained in strength :

(*a*) From D'Annunzio's soldiers, who had returned from Fiume.

(*b*) After the decline in the influence of the Socialists, who failed to seize control of the State during a great strike at Milan in 1920.

94

(*c*) From the organization of a private army, known from their dress as ' Blackshirts.' These men put down disorder in the provinces and helped to break the General Strike of 1922.

(*d*) When it dissociated itself from Republicanism. In 1921 the Fascists, now recognized as a powerful political party, declared their loyalty to the House of Savoy.

(*e*) From the support of peasants, middle-class people, and wealthy industrialists who feared the growth of Socialism.

IV. THE MARCH ON ROME (1922)

At the annual Fascist Congress at Naples in 1922, Mussolini threatened to march his Blackshirts to Rome and seize power if the Government were not handed over to him. In October, 30,000 Fascist soldiers marched in four orderly columns towards Rome. (Mussolini was at Milan.) There was no fighting. The King summoned his Ministers, persuaded them to resign, and then invited Mussolini to form a ministry.

V. MUSSOLINI IN POWER

Mussolini determined (i) to destroy parliamentary government and make himself a dictator—his later aims gradually became clear ; (ii) to make Italy prosperous and self-sufficient ; (iii) to gain respect for Italy as a Great Power.

(*a*) *The Establishment of the Dictatorship* (1922–1925)

During these years Mussolini was engaged in crushing all opposition and making his dictatorship secure.

(i) He destroyed the power of the Italian Parliament by changing the electoral system so that its members were nominated only by the Fascist Party. This constitution came into effect in 1928.

(ii) He ruthlessly punished his opponents by terrorist methods of imprisonment, torture, and exile. The murder of Matteotti, a Socialist deputy, in 1924, excited universal condemnation.

(iii) He established a strict censorship of the Press and curtailed the liberty of the Italians.

By these means Mussolini set up a dictatorship of the Fascist Party. Though his Government curtailed liberty, it was efficient and restored order. All power rested in the Fascist Grand Council of Ministers, of which Mussolini was President.

(*b*) *Economic Reorganization of Italy—the Corporative State*

Mussolini planned to control completely the economic life of the state. He declared that every citizen must serve the interests of the country and not his own selfish ends ; the working classes were forbidden to strike, the employers were ordered to reduce hours of labour or increase wages. For each branch of industry—agriculture, manufacturing, banking, transport, professional services—a separate ' corporation,' representing the employers and employed, determined the conditions of labour.

Much was done to develop Italy's resources :

(i) Improved methods of agriculture and the reclamation of marsh-lands.

(ii) Development of hydro-electric power to overcome the absence of coal.

(iii) Modernization of roads and railways.

(iv) Public works in the cities—the restoration of the monuments of Ancient Rome.

(c) Settlement of the Dispute with the Church

After long negotiations a Concordat was made between Mussolini and the Vatican in 1929. The Italian Government recognized the Vatican City (part of Rome) as an independent state, and the Pope as its temporal sovereign. The Pope at last recognized the Kingdom of Italy, and Rome as its capital.

(d) Foreign Policy of Mussolini

Mussolini won the enthusiastic support of the people by his spirited foreign policy ; he made Italy an active force in European politics.

(i) *Conflict with Yugo-Slavia in the Adriatic.* He settled the dispute with Yugo-Slavia in 1924 and obtained part of Fiume for Italy, the suburb of Susak passing to Yugo-Slavia. He established a protectorate over Albania.

(ii) *Corfu Incident.* In 1923 an Italian general was murdered by a Greek. Failing to get satisfaction from the Greek Government, Mussolini ordered the bombardment of the Greek island of Corfu.

(iii) *The Protector of Austria.* There was a strong movement in Austria for union with Germany. The Austrian dictatorship was maintained by the Heimwehr, a private army which received its arms from Italy. Without Italian support Austria would have been in danger of absorption by Germany.

(iv) *Abyssinia.* To add to his prestige Mussolini sought to extend his empire in Africa, and in 1934 Italy seized Abyssinia. This action brought him into conflict with the League of Nations, which he had never energetically supported.

POST-WAR GERMANY

I. THE WEIMAR REPUBLIC

When the Hohenzollern Empire collapsed in November, 1918, a new republican constitution was drawn up in the town of Weimar. Though there was a President, the most important person was the Chancellor, whose position was similar to that of the British Prime Minister.

From 1919–1930 the Social-Democratic Party was the mainstay of the new Republic. The overwhelming difficulties, political and economic, and especially the odium of having accepted the humiliating terms of the Treaty of Versailles, led to the decline in the party's influence. Its failure to prevent the collapse of the currency in 1923, and the consequent wiping out of bank-balances, cost it the support of the middle classes. From 1924 to 1929 the Republic gained stability, but the prosperity which marked these years was built upon unsound finance (see pp. 83–86), and during the world economic crisis not only the finance and industry, but the political institutions themselves, began to totter. The Social-Democratic Party no longer held the confidence of the people of Germany.

II. THE RISE OF HITLER AND NATIONAL-SOCIALISM

Adolf Hitler, an Austrian Socialist who had fought in the Great War as a private soldier, founded the National-Socialist Party at Munich in 1920. His programme was an attack on the Jews, the profiteers in Germany, the Communists, the Treaty of

Versailles, and the weakness of the Government. He possessed great personal magnetism and hypnotized his listeners, however numerous or hostile, to a belief in his mission to 'save Germany.' His ideas were welcomed by the embittered lower middle class, the big industrialists, and by the peasants all over Germany. He appealed especially to

MAP 42

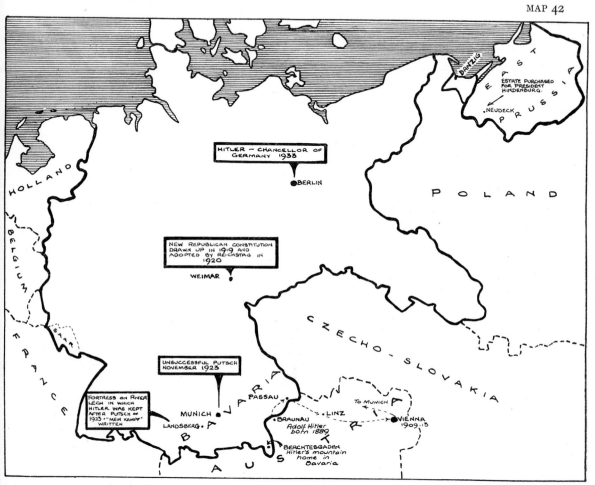

POST-WAR GERMANY

young people, and taught them to glorify their own Teutonic race and believe in its future.

In 1923 he attempted in Munich a revolution, or *putsch*, which was an ignominious failure. He was sent to prison and spent his time writing *Mein Kampf*, which became the authoritative exposition of Nazi policy.

As the economic situation grew worse, the Nazi Party increased its representation in the German Reichstag, and in 1933 the President, Hindenburg, was forced to summon them to power. Hitler became Chancellor. For a time he was forced to accept the support of the Nationalist Party (supporters of the old Imperial *régime*). A mysterious

G

fire which destroyed the Reichstag was alleged to be the work of Communists ; it afforded an excuse for crushing the opposition of Jews and Communists. This was done by a specially trained Nazi force known as the ' Brown Shirts.' Hitler employed the methods of Mussolini with even greater violence and brutality.

In 1934 he no longer desired the assistance of the Nationalist Party. He compelled its members to resign from the Government and destroyed the organization. On the night of June 30 he purged his party in a general massacre of those leaders who, he felt, were not wholehearted supporters. He thus assumed complete authority, summoning the Reichstag only to announce his decisions. He controlled the Press, he attacked the Churches, and set up his dictatorial rule in all the states of Germany. When President Hindenburg died in 1934, Hitler assumed the office of President as well as that of Chancellor.

III. HITLER IN POWER—THE THIRD REICH

Hitler triumphantly justified the hopes of his supporters. He tackled the following problems with great boldness :

(a) *The Restoration of German Self-respect*

By his daring and energetic foreign policy and by organized propaganda he has aroused an overwhelming pride of race in Germany. Racialism has become the German religion. This paganism led to conflict with the Roman Catholic and Protestant Churches.

(b) *Foreign Policy*

With drastic violence Hitler denounced the humiliating conditions imposed on Germany by the Treaty of Versailles. In October, 1933, he withdrew from the Disarmament Conference and gave notice of his intention to leave the League of Nations. In March, 1935, he repudiated the military clauses of the Peace Treaty and began to create a gigantic army based on conscription. At the same time Britain and Germany scrapped the naval clauses of the treaty and came to a new naval arrangement. A year later he repudiated the Locarno Pact, and his armies re-entered the Rhineland.

His avowed aim is the union of all Germanic peoples under National Socialism. This implies the annexation of Austria (effected in March, 1938), Danzig, Memel, as well as parts of Poland, Czecho-Slovakia, and Switzerland.

(c) *Economic Problems and Unemployment*

(i) The great landed estates were divided up and handed over to small farmers.

(ii) Public works, *e.g.*, the construction of new motor-roads, absorbed thousands of the unemployed.

(iii) Labour-camps were instituted to discipline the nation and provide cheap labour.

(iv) National planning has been organized under an economic dictator to enable Germany to become self-sufficient.

SINCE THE PEACE SETTLEMENT

The Union of Socialist Soviet Republics

I. CONSTITUTION

The U.S.S.R. comprises seven republics, all of which are governed by Soviets, or working-class councils. These are Russia, the Ukraine, White Russia, Transcaucasia, and three areas in Turkestan. Of these the most important is the Russian S.S.R., and the capital of the Union is Moscow, in the centre of European Russia.

MAP 43

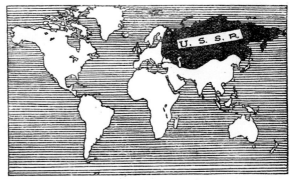

THE UNION OF SOCIALIST SOVIET REPUBLICS

The local Soviets choose delegates to represent themselves in provincial councils; the provincial councils send representatives to the national council, the Congress of the Soviets, which nominally holds supreme power. The real control, however, is in the hands of the leaders of the Communist Party.

II. SUMMARY OF DEVELOPMENT SINCE 1920

(a) *Lenin*

By 1920 the Bolsheviks had cleared the country of the armies of foreign states, and Lenin was in supreme power. His aim was to organize a world revolution, but he had first to reshape Russia itself. Conditions in town and country alike were appalling.

His chief difficulty was to satisfy the peasants, who resisted attempts to confiscate their harvests. Famines in 1920 and 1921 compelled him to make concessions in order to restore some measure of prosperity to the country. By his new economic policy, announced in 1921, a certain amount of private trading was permitted both in town and country.

(b) *Stalin*

On the death of Lenin in 1924, Joseph Stalin, son of a Caucasian cobbler, was the secretary of the Communist Party. He gained the dominant influence in the party and became the dictator of Russia. His aim was to develop the resources of the country and make Russia a powerful state and to improve the unfriendly relations which had existed between her and the other nations of the world. He was prepared to delay the coming of the World Revolution to secure these ends. His chief rival was Trotsky, who opposed this policy and objected to individuals having private rights or property in a Communist state. In 1927 Stalin was sufficiently strong to drive Trotsky and his followers into exile.

(c) *Five-Year Plan*

This grandiose scheme planned the development of Russia's industries, education, and agriculture.

(i) *Industries.* New factories for making tractors, new steel-mills, hydro-electric power-stations, and railways were constructed.

MAP 44

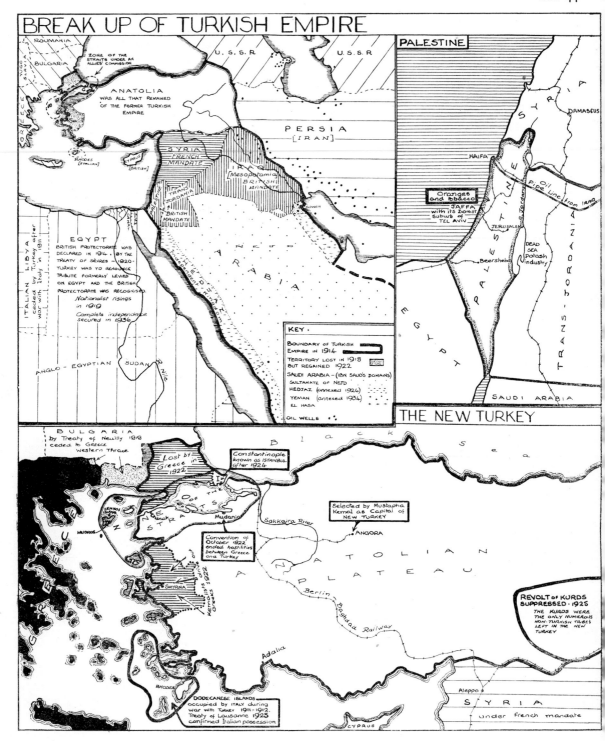

BREAK UP OF TURKISH EMPIRE

ROUMANIA

BULGARIA

ZONE OF THE STRAITS UNDER AN ALLIES COMMISSION

GREECE   SERBIA   YUGO

U.S.S.R.

U.S.S.R.

ANATOLIA
WAS ALL THAT REMAINED
OF THE FORMER TURKISH
EMPIRE

RHODES
[ITALIAN]

CYPRUS
[BRITISH]

PERSIA
[IRAN]

SYRIA
FRENCH
MANDATE

IRAQ
(Mesopotamia)
BRITISH
MANDATE

KUWEIT

TRANS
JORDANIA

PALESTINE BRITISH MANDATE

ITALIAN LIBYA ceded by Turkey after war with Italy in 1911

EGYPT
BRITISH PROTECTORATE WAS
DECLARED IN 1914. BY THE
TREATY OF SÈVRES - 1920 -
TURKEY WAS TO RENOUNCE
TRIBUTE FORMERLY LEVIED
ON EGYPT AND THE BRITISH
PROTECTORATE WAS RECOGNISED.
*Nationalist risings
in 1919*
*Complete independence
secured in 1936*

N E J D

A R A B I A

ANGLO - EGYPTIAN SUDAN   Nile

KEY
BOUNDARY OF TURKISH
EMPIRE IN 1914
TERRITORY LOST IN 1918
BUT REGAINED 1922
SAUDI ARABIA - (IBN SAUD'S DOMAINS)
SULTANATE OF NEJD
HEDJAZ (annexed 1926)
YEMAN (annexed 1934)
EL HASA
OIL WELLS

PALESTINE

SYRIA

DAMASCUS

HAIFA

Oranges and tobacco

JAFFA
with its Zionist
Suburb of
TEL AVIV

Oil Pipe Line from IRAQ

JERUSALEM

DEAD
SEA
Potash
Industry

Beersheba

PALESTINE

TRANS-JORDANIA

EGYPT

SAUDI ARABIA

THE NEW TURKEY

BULGARIA
by Treaty of Neuilly 1919
ceded to Greece
Western Thrace

B l a c k   S e a

Lost by
Greece in
1922

Constantinople
known as ISTANBUL
after 1924

Selected by Mustapha
Kemal as Capital of
NEW TURKEY

LEMNOS

ZONE OF THE STRAITS

MUDROS

Mudania

Sakkaira River

ANGORA

GREECE

Convention of
October 1922
ended hostilities
between Greece
and Turkey

SMYRNA

Atrocities 1922 by Greeks

A N A T O L I A N   P L A T E A U

Berlin

Baghdad Railway

REVOLT of KURDS
SUPPRESSED · 1925
THE KURDS WERE
THE ONLY NUMEROUS
NON-TURKISH TRIBES
LEFT IN THE NEW
TURKEY

RHODES

Adalia

DODECANESE ISLANDS
occupied by ITALY during
war with TURKEY 1911-1912.
Treaty of Lausanne 1923
confirmed Italian possession

CYPRUS

Aleppo

S Y R I A
under french mandate

(ii) *Education.* An attempt was made to educate the Russian people, the majority of whom were illiterate. There was an urgent need for skilled technicians to work the new machines in the factories.

(iii) *Agriculture.* The number of state farms was increased; they were model institutions intended to educate the peasants in the art of better agriculture. The small-holders, the peasants, were encouraged to combine their tiny plots of land and farm the land collectively. The rich peasants (*kulaks*) objected to the collective farms, and in 1929 Stalin determined to destroy them. They were deported to poorer districts or sent to labour-camps.

A second 'five-year plan' was instituted in 1933 to provide by methods of mass production the goods such as clothes, boots, and furniture urgently required by the people.

THE BREAK-UP OF THE TURKISH EMPIRE

I. THE END OF THE OTTOMAN EMPIRE

The Ottoman Empire, ruled by the Sultan, steadily declined in the nineteenth century. Its ruler, the Sultan, was too feeble to maintain his former vast dominions. By 1914 the Christian peoples of the Balkans had won their independence. Over Egypt and the whole of North Africa the Sultan's power was only nominal, for the European Powers had gained control. The corrupt and inefficient rule of the Turks had provoked opposition among the Arabs, and the Great War gave them their opportunity of freeing themselves from Turkish control.

(a) *The Defeat of Turkey* (1918) *and its Effects*

The overthrow of the Turkish armies was complete; all the provinces from the Mediterranean to the Persian Gulf were overrun, and the great cities of Bagdad, Jerusalem, Damascus, and Aleppo were captured. The Turks were forced to acknowledge defeat, and signed an armistice at Mudros in October, 1918. Allied troops occupied Constantinople.

(b) *The Peace Settlement*

It was soon apparent that the task of settling the conflicting claims of the victorious Powers would be very difficult. By secret treaties made during the War, promises of Turkish territory had been made to Russia, Italy, France, Greece, and to the Arabs. The Allied statesmen postponed the settlement of the difficult problem until they had settled the more urgent needs of Europe. They permitted the Greeks, however, to occupy the port of Smyrna in 1919 and supported the occupation by an Allied fleet. This action aroused indignation among the Turks.

(c) *Mustapha Kemel and the Beginning of the New Turkey*

Led by Mustapha Kemel, the hero of Gallipoli, the Turks formed a new Nationalist Party at Angora, in the middle of Anatolia. In January, 1920, the Sultan was forced to summon a Parliament at Constantinople; this Parliament adopted the " National Pact," which demanded " Turkey for the Turks." The Allies protested, and owing to the presence of the British fleet in the Straits, the Sultan was made to repudiate the pact.

(d) The Treaty of Sèvres

The terms of this treaty were published shortly afterwards. It deprived Turkey of all her outlying provinces and even of the fertile plains of Asia Minor. (Greece was to receive the region round Smyrna, and Italy was to receive Adalia and a large tract in the south.) There remained to Turkey only the capital, Constantinople, and separated from this city, by a "neutral zone of the straits," part of the barren plateau of Anatolia.

The Sultan accepted the treaty, but Mustapha Kemel and his Nationalist Party fiercely rejected it. When the Greeks advanced to occupy their new territory they were attacked and decisively beaten by Mustapha Kemel at the Battle of the Sakkaria River. At the end of the War with Greece (1920–1922) the Turks had reoccupied Smyrna. As the Allies were not prepared to send armies to help the Greeks, they were forced to come to terms with the Nationalists; at a Conference at Mudania they consented to revise the terms of the Treaty of Sèvres. Mustapha Kemel then forced the Sultan to abdicate; the Ottoman Empire was abolished, and a new republic was declared with its capital at Angora.

(e) The Treaty of Lausanne (1923)

The demands of Turkey were granted except in Western Thrace. The Turks agreed to demilitarize the straits (*i.e.*, remove the fortifications from the Dardanelles). An exchange of Greek and Turkish populations was provided for. (See note, p. 73.)

II. THE NEW TURKISH REPUBLIC (1923)

In 1923 Mustapha Kemel declared Turkey a Republic and himself its first President. The fallen Sultan had also held the office of Caliph—supreme head of the Mohammedan faith; this office Mustapha Kemel abolished. Kemel, or, as he called himself, the Ghazi, was a fervent nationalist and had no wish to continue Turkey's nominal supremacy over non-Turkish Moslems.

He ruled as a dictator and introduced sweeping changes to modernize and westernize his people :
(a) State schools were built.
(b) The Arab script was abolished and the European (Latin) alphabet made compulsory.
(c) The *purdah* system was abolished, and women were emancipated.
(d) The Fez, symbol of the East, was abolished.
(e) Islam (Mohammedanism) ceased to be the state religion.

These reforms aroused great opposition, which the Ghazi ruthlessly crushed. Determined to complete his internal reforms, he took steps to be on friendly terms with his neighbours. In 1932 Turkey entered the League of Nations. A treaty of non-aggression was made with Russia in 1925, and in 1934 Turkey entered the Balkan Pact. (See Map 39.)

III. THE ARAB PROVINCES OF TURKEY

The Turkish Nationalists did not question the right of the Powers to sever the Arab provinces from Turkey, as they had never claimed territory in which non-Turkish people lived.

The Arab provinces were :

Iraq (Mesopotamia), the lands between the Tigris and the Euphrates ;

Syria, the land between the Mediterranean and the Euphrates :

Palestine, the coastal area to the south of Syria ;

Hedjaz, a strip of Arabia along the Red Sea, including the holy cities of Mecca and Medina ;

Nejd, the desert of Central Arabia.

The Allies were anxious to keep their promises to give the Arabs independence.

(*a*) In 1916 the British Government had agreed to France's acquiring certain rights in Syria in return for French support to British claims in Mesopotamia.

(*b*) In 1917 the Balfour Declaration had promised the Jews a national home in Palestine.

(*c*) Britain was interested in the oil-wells of Iraq as well as the Suez Canal ; occupation of Palestine, which lay north of the Canal, afforded another control of the route to the East.

(*d*) President Wilson had set down in his ' Fourteen Points ' that the nationalities under Turkish rule should have the right to govern themselves.

After much controversy the Allies, without consulting the inhabitants, arranged a division of the territory as follows :

$$\textit{Britain} \text{ secured a mandate over} \left. \begin{cases} \text{Iraq} \\ \text{Palestine} \\ \text{Trans-Jordania} \end{cases} \right\} \text{Syria divided into three parts.}$$

France secured a mandate over North Syria

The independent Kingdom of the Hedjaz, with its capital at Mecca, was ruled by the Sherif Hussein, who claimed overlordship over the rest of Arabia. The Allies underestimated and ignored the Arab national movement led by Ibn Saud in Central Arabia.

IV. AFTER THE SETTLEMENT

The partition of the former Turkish provinces and their allocation to France and Britain has not brought peace to the Middle East. The awakened national spirit of the Arabs has caused almost continuous unrest.

(*a*) *Ibn Saud*

This leader of the strict sect of Moslems was the ruler of the Nejd, the desert of Central Arabia. In 1932 he overran the Red Sea provinces which had been declared the independent Kingdom of the Hedjaz. In 1934 he annexed Yemen. He thereby became ruler of Arabia from Red Sea to Persian Gulf.

(*b*) *The French in Syria*

When the French occupied Syria in 1920 they declared the Arab Kingdom set up by Feisal in 1918 at Damascus abolished. They divided the country into five separate provinces under different administrators. The French selected Arabs for these posts, and the natives ruled independently, though they received advice from French officials. There was a common currency, and the whole of Syria formed a single customs area.

The division of the country was one of the chief grievances of the Arabs. A rebellion broke out in 1925 among the Druse tribes, and open revolt in Damascus followed. Unrest which led frequently to armed rising prevailed, until finally in 1936 a settlement was made by which Syria was to become an independent state.

(c) The British in Palestine

When the British accepted the mandate to control Palestine they endeavoured to carry out the promise made in the Balfour Declaration to make the country a home for the Jews. This policy was dictated partly from motives of idealism and partly as a bid to secure the support of the Jews of the world during the War. The Arabs who lived in Palestine were bitterly opposed to the project. They refused to accept the mandate, and all attempts to introduce measures of self-government have failed because the two peoples have refused to co-operate.

Economically the country has prospered; the Jews have invested capital in the country, and irrigation schemes have greatly benefited its agriculture. In spite of the admitted fact that they were better off, the Arabs continued their agitation. Violent anti-Jewish riots broke out in Jerusalem in 1929, and the country has remained in a state of turmoil and distress almost continuously up to 1937. A proposal to partition the country was made by a visiting British commission in 1936, but was opposed alike by Jews and Arabs.

(d) The British in Trans-Jordania

Trans-Jordania extends from the River Jordan across the Syrian Desert towards the Euphrates. The firm rule of the territory prevents raiding tribes from the Arabian Desert from entering the agricultural lands of Palestine. The state is governed by a member of the Sherif family, but with the advice of a British resident who is the real ruler (*cf.* native states in India). British soldiers defend the country and the pipe-line which carries oil across the desert from Iraq to Haifa on the Mediterranean.

(e) The British in Iraq

When the British Mandate was granted in 1923, the Iraqis revolted; they had hoped for complete independence after the overthrow of the Turks. In 1921 the British made Feisal, one of the leaders of the Arab revolt, King of Iraq and withdrew the British army from Mesopotamia, leaving a detachment of the Air Force to police the country.

The new state had difficulties with:

(i) *Turkey:* The Turks claimed Mosul because of its Kurdish population. The Kurds themselves wanted the independence they had been promised at Sèvres in 1920. Mosul was the important centre of the Iraq Petroleum Company's oil-wells. In 1925 a League Commission assigned Mosul to Iraq.

(ii) *Ibn Saud*, the ruler of Arabia, who caused trouble in the south.

(iii) *Persia*, where the people were of a different Moslem sect.

In 1927 Britain acknowledged Iraq as an independent state, and in 1932 the new country was admitted to the League of Nations.

V. THE BRITISH IN EGYPT

Britain had exercised influence in Egypt since her purchase of the controlling interest in the Suez Canal (1875). In the early years of the twentieth century a nationalist movement had grown up ; it was strongly opposed to British interference. On the outbreak of War Britain refused to recognize any longer the nominal suzerainty of Turkey over Egypt and proclaimed her protectorate.

At the end of the War the nationalist agitation increased. The Wafd Party, led by Zaghul Pasha, demanded complete independence ; the British wished to reserve military control, as they were interested only in the security of the Suez route to the East.

In 1930 King Fuad of Egypt set up a dictatorship, but it was not until 1935 that agreement was reached with Britain to the satisfaction of the Nationalist Party.

THE FAR EAST

I. CHINA

From the time when Britain first forced China to open her ports to British trade in 1842, European nations developed their own interests in China. Securing trade concessions from the Chinese Government by treaty, they gradually extended their control over the financial interests of the country until the sovereign power of the Chinese Government was threatened.

(a) The Chinese Republic (1912)

At last the Chinese awakened to the danger, and inspired by the teaching of Dr Sun Yat Sen, they rose and overthrew their rulers, the Manchu Emperors. This was the first stage in a revolution which in a few years transformed China. The Chinese have broken from the traditions of the past. They have accepted western ideas, and there has grown up opposition to foreign exploitation.

The overthrow of the old rulers led to disorder ; the country was distracted by civil strife. Military governors—' war-lords '—in the Provinces made themselves semi-independent, although until 1916 a dictator ruling from Peking held the Republic together nominally.

(b) Effects of the Great War and the Peace

On the outbreak of the Great War Japan seized the opportunity to wrest from the Government at Peking the acceptance of ' Twenty-one Points '—demands which threatened to make China a dependency of Japan. They included a claim to control South Manchuria and Inner Mongolia.

China had declared war on Germany in 1917, and was represented at the Peace Conference not only by delegates from the Government at Peking, but by representatives of a Nationalist (*Kuo-Min-Tang*—National People's Party) Government at Canton, the followers of Dr Sun Yat Sen. The Nationalist delegation obstinately claimed freedom from foreign control and a revision of the Concessions Treaties. Japan claimed the right to inherit the former German concessions in China, and Britain and France supported her. Japan thus received the former German rights in the Province of Shantung and a mandate over former German islands in the Pacific north of the equator. The Chinese Government refused to acknowledge these terms.

(c) Increasing Power of the Kuo-Min-Tang : the Nationalist Revolution (1924–1927)

In 1924 the Government of the Kuo-Min-Tang sought the help of the Soviet Government. Their aim was to unite China ; they had no belief in Communist ideas, but

105

MAP 45

THE FAR EAST

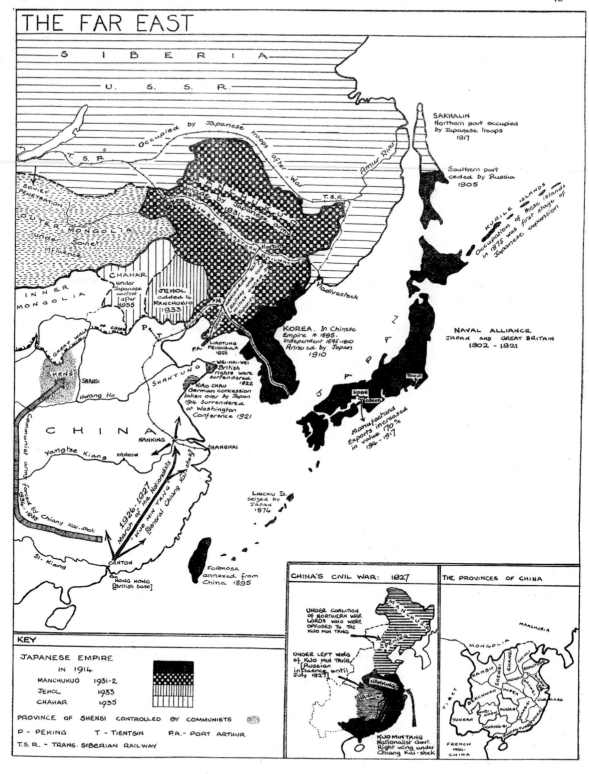

S I B E R I A

U. S. S. R.

Occupied by Japanese troops after War

T. S. R.

SOVIET PENETRATION

OUTER MONGOLIA under Soviet influence

INNER MONGOLIA

CHAHAR under Japanese control after 1935

JEHOL added to MANCHUKUO 1933

MANCHUKUO occupied by Japanese army 1931-2

Harbin

Amur River

T. S. R.

Vladivostock

SAKHALIN
Northern part occupied by Japanese troops 1917

Southern part ceded by Russia 1905

KURILE ISLANDS
Occupation of these islands in 1875 was first stage of Japanese expansion

GREAT WALL OF CHINA

SHENSI SHANSI

Hwang Ho

Communist army forced by Chiang Kai-shek 1934-1935

P T

LIAOTUNG PENINSULA 1905

WEI-HAI-WEI British rights were surrendered 1922

KIAO CHAU German concession taken over by Japan 1914 Surrendered at Washington Conference 1921

SHANTUNG

KOREA. In Chinese Empire to 1895. Independent 1895-1910 Annexed by Japan 1910

NAVAL ALLIANCE
JAPAN AND GREAT BRITAIN 1902 - 1921

TOKIO
KOBE
OSAKA

Manufactures Exports increased 170% in value 1914-1917

C H I N A

Yangtse Kiang HANKOW

NANKING

SHANGHAI

1926-1927 March of the Nationalists
KUO MIN TANG [General Chiang Kai-shek]

Si- Kiang

CANTON

HONG KONG [British base]

FORMOSA annexed from China 1895

LIUCHIU Is. seized by JAPAN 1876

KEY

JAPANESE EMPIRE
IN 1914
MANCHUKUO 1931-2
JEHOL 1933
CHAHAR 1935

PROVINCE OF SHENSI CONTROLLED BY COMMUNISTS

P - PEKING T - TIENTSIN P.A. - PORT ARTHUR

T.S.R. - TRANS- SIBERIAN RAILWAY

CHINA'S CIVIL WAR: 1927

UNDER COALITION OF NORTHERN WAR LORDS WHO WERE OPPOSED TO THE KUO MIN TANG

UNDER LEFT WING OF KUO MIN TANG [Russian influence] until July 1927

NANKING
HANKOW

KUO MIN TANG Nationalist Govt. Right wing under Chiang Kai-shek

THE PROVINCES OF CHINA

MANCHURIA

MONGOLIA

KANSU SHENSI SHANSI CHIHLI SHANTUNG

TIBET SZECHWAN HONAN ANHUI KIANGSU

HUPEH CHEKIANG

SHEN-CHOW HUNAN KIANGSI FUKIEN

YUNNAN KWANG-SI KWANGTUNG

FRENCH INDO-CHINA

under Russian influence they began to organize their party on Soviet lines and trained an army under Russian officers. A minority group in the Kuo-Min-Tang wanted to create a Communist State in China, but they were not important until after 1927.

On the death of Sun Yat Sen in 1925, General Chiang Kai-Shek, the foremost military leader, taking advantage of the weakness of the Government at Peking and the disunion among the Northern war-lords, carried out the bold plan of extending Nationalist influence from Canton, in South China, to the Yangtse Valley, in Central China. With comparatively little effort the central provinces fell to his victorious army, which seized Hankow, the principal city and port of the Middle Yangtse, and afterwards took Shanghai, the principal port of China, and Nanking.

Thus, on the completion of this 'Northern Expedition' of Chiang Kai-Shek in 1927, China was divided under the rule of :

(i) A Northern Government at Peking ; its effective authority was limited to the Northern provinces. This was the Government recognized by Western Europe and to which foreign ambassadors were accredited.

(ii) A Nationalist (Kuo-Min-Tang) Government at Hankow and Canton, which controlled Central and South China.

(iii) Military governors who ruled the remote provinces and were almost independent.

(d) Chiang Kai-Shek's Coup d'État (1927)

The Hankow Government was strongly Communist. When its anti-foreign policy led to outrages in Nanking and Shanghai, Chiang Kai-Shek opposed it and set up his own rule at Nanking ('southern capital'). Civil war broke out between the two factions, but Chiang Kai-Shek overthrew the Hankow Government and expelled the Russian advisers. Acknowledged leader of the Kuo-Min-Tang, Chiang Kai-Shek marched north, captured Peking (renaming it Peiping—'northern peace'), and declared himself dictator of all China, of which Nanking became the new capital. Chiang Kai-Shek was then recognized by the British Government.

(e) Difficulties of Chiang Kai-Shek

(i) *The growth of Communism among the peasantry*. Though able to crush the movement in the cities, he failed to suppress its growth among the peasants. At first strong in the Province of Kiangsi, the Soviet supporters were forced to move to the remote Province of Shensi, where a Soviet Government was established.

(ii) *The insubordination of the outlying provinces*. The most important of the semi-independent war-lords was the ruler of Manchuria—the three 'northern provinces' of the old Chinese Empire.

(iii) *The increasing aggression of Japan*. After 1931 it became increasingly manifest that Japan was embarking on a policy of aggression against China. Ostensibly to protect her treaty rights in Manchuria, which she claimed had been violated by the Chinese, and in reality to seize land, minerals, and a vast potential market for her manufactures, Japan invaded Manchuria in the autumn of 1931. China appealed to the League of Nations, but the Japanese refused to withdraw, and within a year they proclaimed an independent state—Manchukuo—ruled by the deposed Manchu Emperor, with the aid of Japanese advisers and supported by the Japanese army. Lord Lytton,

107

MAP 46

IRELAND BEFORE TREATY

AFTER TREATY

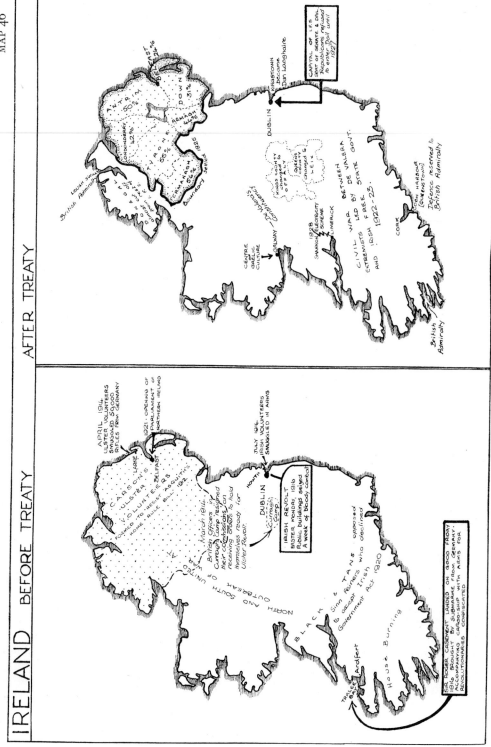

PERCENTAGES SHOWN IN NORTHERN IRELAND SHOW PROPORTION OF ROMAN CATHOLICS instructed by the League to report on the situation, censured Japan, and the League adopted his report in 1933. In protest Japan withdrew from the League and continued her conquest of the North of China in Jehol and Inner Mongolia.

The continued aggression of Japan in China proper led Chiang Kai-Shek to ally himself with the more extreme Communist party (1937).

II. JAPAN

(a) The Great War and After

In 1902, confronted by the aggressive expansion of Russia, Japan concluded an alliance with England. Adhering to this treaty, Japan declared war on Germany in 1914, but her only contribution to the Allied cause was the capture of the German territory in Shantung Province.

Japan emerged from the War one of the Great Powers. While her competitors in Western Europe had been busy with the provision of war-supplies, Japanese manufacturers had enormously expanded their exports and had captured important markets all over the world. Nevertheless, she was faced by many difficulties.

(i) *Political.* She was diplomatically isolated : America was antagonistic ; Russia in arms against her ; China was hostile ; and the Alliance with England no longer certain.

(ii) *Economic.* Her position was unsound. A slump in trade followed the period of artificial war-prosperity, and difficulties were increased by the raising of tariff-walls against her manufactures and the boycott imposed by China. Expenditure on armaments was heavy, and naval competition with the U.S.A. a burden.

(b) The Washington Conference (1921–1922)

A Nine-Power Conference summoned in the U.S.A. capital to deal with Far-Eastern problems and naval armaments resulted in the signing of two very important agreements :

(i) The Powers promised to respect the sovereignty and independence of China, and to maintain the principle of equal opportunities for commerce for all nations.

(ii) The three principal naval powers—Britain, U.S.A., and Japan—agreed to restrict naval competition in certain classes of warships and settled on the ratios 5 : 5 : 3 respectively.

At this conference Japan restored the former German territory in Shantung to China, and promised to withdraw her armies from Soviet territory in Siberia.

N.B.—Japan adhered to the Washington provisions until 1931, when her industry and trade suffered badly during the whole economic crisis (see pp. 83–86). As a consequence of the dissatisfaction which prevailed, the militarist clique was able to dictate the foreign policy of the Japanese Government, and aggression in China followed.

IRELAND

Although most of the grievances which had embittered the Irish people in the nineteenth century had been rectified, the greatest obstacle to friendly relations with England remained—the refusal of the British Government to grant home rule. The Conservative Party, during a long period of power, had adopted the policy of extending beneficial reforms to improve the economic prosperity of the people, but they had not succeeded in overcoming antagonism to British rule.

1. BEFORE THE TREATY OF 1921

(a) *Rise of Sinn Fein* (1905)

Resistance grew among the young generation, who were impatient of the futile efforts of the Irish Nationalist Party in the British Parliament. Originating in a literary movement and the reviving interest in the Erse language, a new political party was organized by a journalist, Arthur Griffith, which took as its motto *Sinn Fein* (' Ourselves alone '). It worked for a completely free Irish Parliament.

(b) *Irish Reform Bill* (1912)

The Irish Nationalist Party held the balance of power in the Parliament of 1910, and John Redmond, the leader of the party, secured the promise of home rule as the price of his party's support of the Liberal administration. When the Home Rule Bill was introduced in 1912, it had little chance of success, because it was opposed by :

(i) The Unionists, who were prepared to take up arms to uphold the established order in Ireland.

(ii) The Protestants of Ulster fiercely resisted an independence which might put them under Roman Catholic domination. In 1912 they signed a solemn covenant to resist home rule.

Passed by the House of Commons, it was rejected by the Lords, though as a consequence of the Parliament Act of 1911, it became law in 1914.

The Ulstermen, led by Sir Edward Carson, formed a volunteer force and began to drill openly ; the Nationalists organized a similar force in the south. The situation was serious. Army officers stationed at Curragh Camp were known to be sympathetic to Ulster. There was open defiance of the Government both in the north and south. (*N.B.* the Larne and Howth episodes—smuggling in arms from abroad.)

(c) *Great War*

On the outbreak of the War the Home Rule Bill was suspended, and the Irish Nationalists declared their loyalty. Irishmen from all parts of the country enlisted in the British army. The pro-British policy of the Nationalists drove many of its supporters into the Sinn Fein movement, which, in 1916, planned an armed rising in Dublin. They seized the public buildings and proclaimed a Republic. German support for this insurrection was expected (*N.B.* the landing of Sir Roger Casement at Tralee). This Easter Rising of 1916 was put down with great severity. The influence of the Irish Nationalist Party waned, and in the 1918 election the Sinn Fein Party captured all the seats in Southern Ireland.

(d) ' *Irish Republic* ' (1919)

Refusing to sit in the British Parliament, the Sinn Feiners met in Dublin in a Dail (Parliament) and proclaimed the Republic of Ireland. Eamon de Valera was elected President. They elected their own ministers, set up their own law-courts, and disregarded the authority of the British Parliament altogether. Although severe measures were taken and the Dail was suppressed, order could not be restored. In 1920 a new Act provided for the establishment of two Parliaments, one for Ulster, and the other for the rest of Ireland. It satisfied the people of Ulster, and the Northern Parliament was opened in 1921.

The Southern Irish, however, resisted. They attacked the Royal Irish Constabulary (the police force), and a reign of terror began. The British Government sent out a special force of armed police, known as the 'Black and Tans,' who resorted to the same terrorist methods as their opponents.

II. THE TREATY OF 1921

By this treaty made between the British Government and the more moderate Sinn Fein leaders, Michael Collins and Arthur Griffith, it was agreed that South Ireland should receive the independent status of a British Dominion, a Governor-General being appointed to represent the Crown. It was to be known as the Irish Free State. (Like other Dominions, it was represented in the League of Nations.) Northern Ireland retained its autonomy. The Sinn Fein Parliament accepted the Treaty in 1922, but Mr de Valera announced his intention to resist until a Republic had been set up. The Irish Parliament drew up its own Constitution. Mr Cosgrave was elected President. Further civil strife followed, and it was not until 1923 that order was restored.

The Republican candidates for the Free State Dail at first refused to take any oath of allegiance and could not therefore sit in Parliament. In 1927 De Valera and his friends entered the Dail. In 1932 they united with the Labour Party and overthrew the Cosgrave Government.

III. AFTER THE TREATY OF 1921

(a) *Work of the Cosgrave Government* (1922–1932)

The Government began the work of reorganization. Relations with Great Britain were comparatively good. English capital supported the development of industry in Ireland. A measure of prosperity was regained after six years of almost continuous disorder. In 1925 more harmonious relations were settled with Northern Ireland by a settlement of the boundary question.

(b) *Work of the De Valera Government from* 1932.

In 1932 Mr de Valera established what was a virtual dictatorship. He had not changed his republican views. He wanted a complete break with England. He attacked the position of the Governor-General and abolished the oath of allegiance to the King. He repudiated the agreement made in the 1921 Treaty to repay the land-annuities—sums of money advanced by Britain to help Irish farmers buy their lands. The British Government retaliated by the imposition of prohibitive duties on Irish agricultural products.

The Irish Free State's policy was to make Ireland self-supporting. It therefore fostered schemes for introducing new industries, developing the national resources, *e.g.*, peat. The infant industries were helped by the protection of high tariffs. The agricultural interests suffered in spite of Government grants, as their only possible market is Great Britain.

Britain since the War

I. DIFFICULTIES

(a) *Economic Difficulties : Post-War Depression*

Britain has suffered more than any other country from trade depression since the War. Foreign competitors have taken many of her markets for manufactured goods, and the decline in world trade has affected the prosperity of her shipping-industry. She had to bear the greatest share in the cost of the War, and the National Debt increased to become a real burden. Heavy taxation increased the difficulties of industry. The most obvious result of the depression was a fluctuating, but always heavy, volume of unemployment. About one man in every six has been continuously out of work. Whole regions—the ' special areas '—are in a semi-derelict condition.

(b) *Industrial Unrest*

The standard of living improved enormously during the War, and the working classes were determined to resist any reduction in their wages. Great unrest prevailed, and disputes were frequent. Between the years 1919–1926 the unions of railwaymen, transport-workers, and miners worked closely together in a ' triple alliance.'

Increasing difficulty in the mining-industry led to the appointment of the Sankey Commission in 1919, but the Government's refusal to nationalize the mines and the owners' reluctance to grant the miners' demands for higher wages led to a strike in 1926. The miners were supported by a sympathetic strike of the workers in the chief industries of the country. It was Britain's first experience of a ' General Strike '; starvation faced the country ; the Baldwin Government dealt with the difficult situation firmly. Public opinion opposed the strikers, and volunteers came to the aid of the Government. After a week the Trade Union leaders were forced to order their members back to work.

The results of the General Strike were :

(i) A weakening of the power of the Trade Unions financially, for the strike had been a drain on their resources, and legally, for the State regarded the General Strike as a challenge to its authority, and in 1927 the Trades Dispute and Trade Unions Act was passed. This measure considerably restricted the power of the Unions ; it made illegal sympathetic strikes and those intended to intimidate the Government, while other provisions hampered the financial resources of the Unions.

(ii) The stoppage of work throughout the country was a national disaster at a time when Britain was struggling to retain her hold on the markets of the world. The miners gained nothing ; their strike lasted seven months, and when their Union funds were exhausted they were forced to return to work at lower wages.

(c) *Political Difficulties : Ineffectiveness of the Party System*

Party politics were discarded during the War, and the Coalition Government continued until 1922. In the meantime the Liberal Party had declined in influence owing to internal divisions, while the Labour Party had taken its place as the Opposition Party.

The efficiency of the party system was impaired :

(i) The existence of three parties prevented the emergence of a powerful Government. One party could not obtain a clear majority over the other two. There were three elections within two years (1922–1924).

(ii) In 1918 the Labour Party had adopted a Socialist programme: A party system cannot be satisfactorily run if the opposing parties hold fundamentally opposite views, yet this was the situation which now developed.

(d) Imperial Difficulties: Growth of Nationalism within the Empire

(i) *Ireland.* See Map 46 and notes on pp. 109–111.

(ii) *India.* This was the most difficult of all the imperial problems which faced the British Government. During the nineteenth century much had been done to improve the prosperity of India, and at the beginning of the twentieth century steps were taken to meet the demand for self-government.

During the War India loyally supported the Empire and was represented at the Peace Conference. Here Indian representatives saw the rights of self-government, which were denied to them, lavishly bestowed on other nations.

After the War the nationalist agitation grew among both Hindus and Moslems. The British Government attempted to satisfy the agitators by a new India Act in 1919 (Chelmsford-Montagu Reforms), a limited measure by which responsible government was granted in the Provinces but not in the Central Government; the reforms applied only to British India, the native states being unaffected.

The Indians were not satisfied, and disturbances grew frequent, especially in the Punjab. In 1919, at Amritsar, General Dyer ordered his troops to fire on an unruly mob; this violent act considerably increased the natives' resentment. Their principal spokesman, Gandhi, adopted the method of 'passive resistance,' and he encouraged the Hindus to refuse to co-operate with the British Government. They boycotted British goods, refused to teach in British schools, and ignored the British Courts. They were imprisoned but offered no resistance.

Gandhi's programme included :

the development of hand-weaving among the peasants ;

the abolition of drugs and spirits ;

the granting of increased freedom to Hindu women ;

the co-operation of Hindus and Moslems ; and

the breaking down of the 'caste-system,' as it affected the 'Untouchables '— *i.e.,* the lowest class of the Hindus, who had been debarred from the communal life of India ; they were banned from the temples and were not allowed to use the drinking-wells of villages.

In 1926 the British Government sent a commission to India under the chairmanship of Sir John Simon. The report, although suggesting further reforms, was not acceptable to Gandhi and his followers. In 1930 the Government summoned a Round Table Conference in London. As a result of this meeting a new India Act was passed in 1935, the principal features of which are (*a*) the federation of British India and the native Indian States, (*b*) the granting of full self-government in the Provinces and a further step towards it in the Central Government.

(iii) *Egypt.* See Map 44 and notes on pp. 104–105.

(iv) *Self-governing Dominions.* The four self-governing Dominions, Canada, South Africa, Australia, and New Zealand, had acquired their freedom and independence

H

before the War, yet there remained many nominal and legal ties which bound them to the mother country. In 1931 Great Britain acknowledged, by the Statute of Westminster (1931), the complete independence of these self-governing dominions and their equality with Britain. The British Commonwealth of Nations is united by their common loyalty to the Crown.

(v) *Mandated Territories.* See Map 36 and notes on pp. 77–79.

II. RISE OF THE LABOUR PARTY

The first Labour Government came into office after the General Election of 1924. It had to depend on the support of the Liberal Party. Though it handled foreign policy successfully, it was unable to introduce any far-reaching socialist measures. A combination of the Conservatives and Liberals drove the Labour Government from office a year later.

In 1929 the Labour Party returned to office. Though stronger, it still had to rely upon the Liberals for support. Moreover, it came into office at the beginning of the world economic crisis (see pp. 85–86). The refusal of the majority of the Cabinet to consider definite economy measures led to a split in the Labour ranks; the Prime Minister (Ramsay Macdonald) and a few friends combined with the Conservatives and some Liberals to form a new National Ministry, while the remaining leaders of the Labour Party led the Opposition.

III. SOCIAL AND ADMINISTRATIVE REFORMS

(a) Formation of New Ministries

In order to deal more effectively with the problems of national insurance against sickness and unemployment, housing, co-ordinated transport, new Government Departments have been created—*e.g.*, the Ministries of Health, Labour, and Transport.

(b) Extension of Franchise

By Acts in 1918 and 1928 the franchise was extended. The Representation of the People Act (1918) gave all men over twenty-one years and all women over thirty who were householders or the wives of householders the right to vote. In 1928 the franchise was extended to all women over twenty-one years.

(c) National Planning and State Socialism

Successive Governments have shrunk from the complete nationalization of British industries and agriculture. Nevertheless, steps in this direction have been taken— *e.g.*, the railways have been co-ordinated into four groups; the Central Electricity Board has been planned to ensure a uniformly cheap supply of electric current; the British Broadcasting Corporation has a monopoly of wireless broadcasting. Schemes to assist farmers and revive our declining agriculture include (i) subsidies for growing particular crops, *e.g.*, sugar-beet and wheat; (ii) marketing boards to organize the production and distribution of farming-products, *e.g.*, milk and pigs; and (iii) quotas and tariffs which restricted the import of foreign agricultural products, *e.g.*, Danish bacon.

(d) *Re-introduction of Protection*

Britain had been the leader of the free-trade movement in the nineteenth century, and all attempts before the War to introduce schemes which would tax foreign goods and give preference to home and imperial products had failed. After the War the outlook of British people changed ; no longer was there a market for British manufacturers all over the world, and the Conservative Ministry of 1922 introduced a limited measure of protection to certain industries, such as artificial silk and motor-cars, by the Safeguarding of Industries Act (1921). After the slump in trade which followed the economic crisis in 1932, the new National Government introduced a full measure of protection—a duty of 10 per cent. was introduced on a whole range of manufactured and semi-manufactured goods from foreign countries.

At the Ottawa Conference of Britain and the Dominions in 1932 the main topic of consideration was 'imperial preference.' Britain undertook to give greater advantages to the Dominions than to other countries, and in return she gained minor concessions. Canada made slight reductions in her favour, and Australia raised the tariffs on goods of foreign nations.

Aerial Developments during and after the War

Although the Wright brothers had flown their biplane in 1903, little advance was made in aeronautics until Bleriot crossed the Channel in 1909, and aviation was still in its infancy in 1914. Nevertheless, aircraft played no small part in the naval and military operations of the War, which stimulated a technical advance to a remarkable degree. By 1918 aeroplanes were regularly put to the following uses :

(a) *Reconnaissance* of enemy movements—*e.g.*, the discovery of Kluck's threat to the British left wing at Mons.

(b) *Artillery observation ;* signals informed gunners how their shots were falling.

(c) *Bombing* enemy towns to destroy morale and disorganize supply of munitions.

(d) *Locating submarines.*

(e) *Fighting ;* to prevent enemy planes from fulfilling above services.

(f) *Machine-gunning* advancing troops—*e.g.*, aeroplanes helped to stem the German advance in 1918.

After the War the financial support afforded by most Governments and the competitive flying for prizes and records provided encouragement to aviators and aircraft designers. The following landmarks should be noted :

1919. Alcock and Brown first crossed the Atlantic in a non-stop flight.
Ross Smith first flew from England to Australia.
First serious air-mail service (England to the Continent).
1920. Van Ryneveld flew from London to Cape Town (new machines at Cairo and Bulawayo).
1924. American army flight round the world.
1926. Byrd flew to the North Pole.
1929. Byrd flew to the South Pole.
1931. Australian air-mail started.
1933. Imperial Airways Ltd. carried 60,000 passengers and 8,000,000 letters.

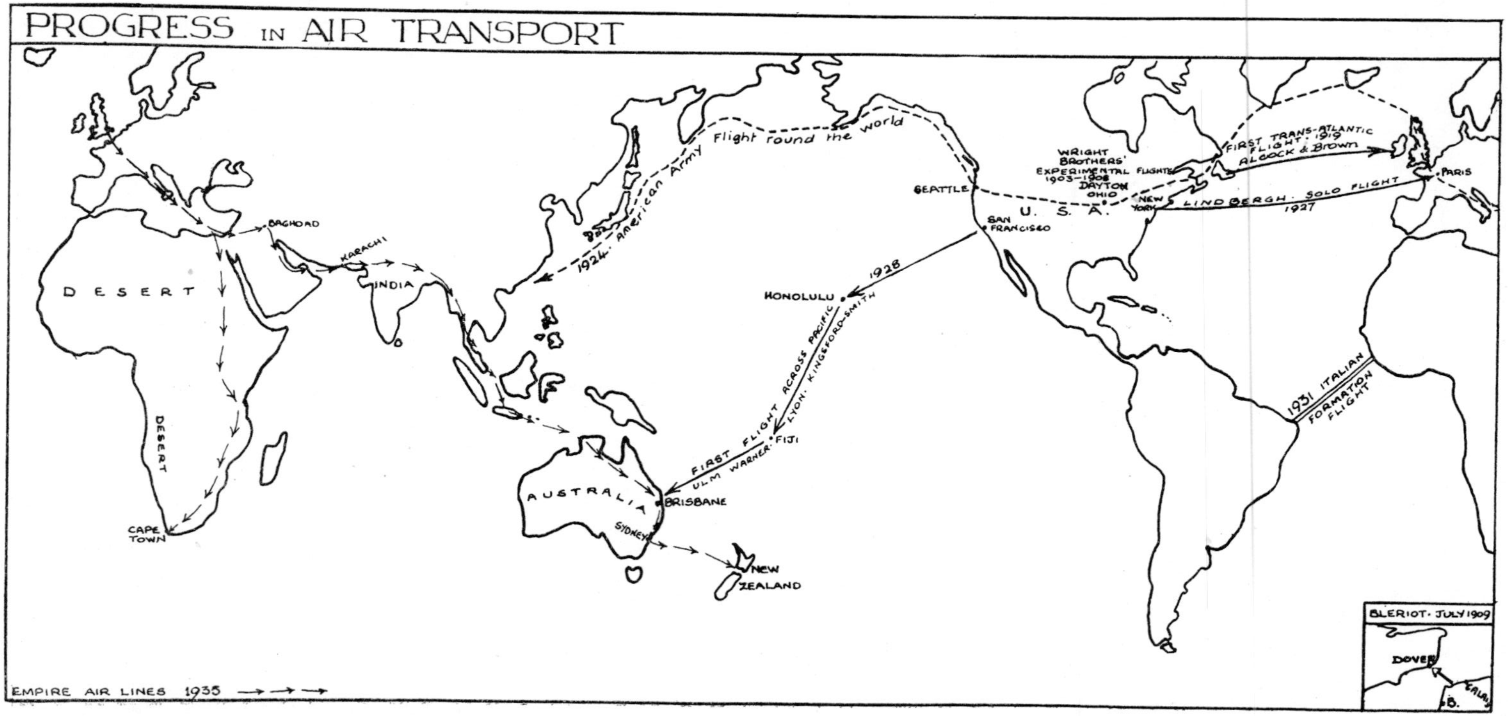

MAP 47

PROGRESS IN AIR TRANSPORT

BLERIOT. JULY 1909

DOVER
ENGLAND

PARIS

FIRST TRANS-ATLANTIC 1919
ALCOCK & BROWN

NEW YORK

LINDBERGH. SOLO FLIGHT 1927

WRIGHT BROTHERS'
EXPERIMENTAL FLIGHTS
1903-1908
DAYTON
OHIO

U. S. A.

SAN FRANCISCO

SEATTLE

Flight round the world

1924 AMERICAN

1931 ITALIAN
FORMATION
FLIGHT

HONOLULU 1928

FLIGHT ACROSS PACIFIC
LYON. KINGSFORD-SMITH.

FIRST ACROSS PACIFIC
ULM. KINGSFORD-SMITH

BRISBANE

AUSTRALIA

SYDNEY

NEW
ZEALAND

BAGDAD

KARACHI

INDIA

DESERT

DESERT

CAPE
TOWN

EMPIRE AIR LINES 1935 ⟶

1934. Scott and Black flew from Mildenhall to Australia in three days.

1937. U.S.A. and Britain began a regular passenger-service across the Atlantic.

In addition to record-breaking flights but largely as a result of these, steady advance has been made in the range, carrying-capacity, and reliability of aeroplanes. The development of airships has suffered from a sequence of serious disasters. A great amount of work has been done in land-survey, the establishment of airports, and the provision of meteorological information upon which aviators depend. In addition to passenger and commercial flying, aeroplanes have been used for aerial survey, fire-patrol in forests, ice-patrol in the North Atlantic, navigation in the New Russian Arctic, and for spraying crops against disease and insect pests.

THE LEAGUE OF NATIONS

During the nineteenth century the idea of submitting difficult problems to arbitration had been accepted (*e.g.*, the Hague Court), yet there was no existing organization sufficiently strong to stop nations from going to war in defence of what they considered their rights.

President Wilson's plan of a society of sovereign states united to preserve the peace of the world by providing the permanent machinery to settle differences was the most important suggestion which engaged the attention of the peace-makers at Versailles in 1919.

I. THE COVENANT

Each member of the League of Nations promised to submit disputes to the League before taking up arms, to uphold international law, and to respect treaty-obligations in order to achieve international peace and security.

II. ORGANIZATION OF THE LEAGUE

(*a*) *The Assembly*

This comprised the delegates of all the member states. It met only once a year to discuss matters affecting the peace of the world.

(*b*) *The Council*

This comprised representatives of the Great Powers and four (later nine) representatives of the secondary states. The council met whenever any particular problem arose that demanded the League's attention. A unanimous vote was required for important decisions.

(*c*) *The Secretariat*

This was the permanent institution at Geneva, in Switzerland, consisting of salaried officials who did the work of preparing the business for discussion.

III. WORK OF THE LEAGUE

(a) *The Preservation of World Peace*

(i) Disputes which concerned the legal interpretation of treaties or of international law were referred to the Permanent Court of International Justice at the Hague.

(ii) Other disputes were first referred to the council to see if they could persuade the parties to agree to a settlement. If not, they named the offending state and called on the other members of the League to apply 'sanctions'[1] against her.

The League machinery has been used to settle many disputes, among which are : The dispute between Greece and Italy over the Corfu incident (see p. 96).

MAP 48

THE AALAND ISLANDS DISPUTE

The claim of Sweden and Finland to the Aaland Islands ;

The settlement of the boundary between Germany and Poland in Upper Silesia (see Map 37) ;

The claim of Turkey and Iraq to the Mosul area (see Map 44) ; and the settlement of boundaries in South America between Peru and Colombia and between Bolivia and Paraguay.

Nevertheless, the League failed to stop the war between Greece and Turkey in 1922 (see Map 44), the Polish seizure of Vilna in 1923 (see Map 37), the French invasion of the Ruhr (see Map 38), the Japanese invasion of Manchuria in 1931 (see Map 45), or the Italian conquest of Abyssinia in 1935–1936 (see Map 41).

Reasons for Its Weakness

(i) Certain Great Powers were not members of the League—U.S.A. and, in the years immediately after the War, Germany and Russia.

(ii) The machinery of the League cannot be effective unless the member states will consent to some curtailment of their sovereign powers, just as the laws of a country will not work if every citizen claims the right to do just as he pleases. The individual forgoes his rights willingly for the sake of the community and so must the member states of the League of Nations. At present they will not admit any loss of their sovereign rights.

(iii) The Powers thought that even the declaration of economic sanctions would lead to war against the offending state. They were reluctant to take any step which might embroil them in naval or military action.

(iv) The League Covenant formed part of each of the Peace Treaties and was associated in the minds of the defeated with the penal clauses imposed on them.

---

[1] 'Sanctions' is a legal expression implying penalty. Sanctions could be economic, *i.e.*, the other countries would not trade with the offender—or military, *i.e.*, the powers would unite to fight her.

(b) Minorities, Mandates, Disputed Territories

Commissions appointed by the League watched the treatment given to national minorities.

The League received annual reports from the mandatory powers and criticized their administration of the mandated territories ; *e.g.*, Great Britain was censured for her failure to reconcile the Jews and Arabs in Palestine.

The Saar Territory remained under the control of the League for fifteen years after the Peace Settlement. The free city of Danzig was also under the jurisdiction of the League.

(c) Reduction of Armaments

Repeated attempts were made by the League to reduce armaments. The most successful was the Washington Conference of 1920–1922 (see p. 109). An attempt to secure the limitation of armaments at the Disarmament Conference (1922–1924) completely failed.

(d) Amelioration of Social Problems

(i) A subsidiary organization of the League—the International Labour Office—considered labour problems, such as the conditions of work in dangerous trades, hours of labour, health of working people.

(ii) Commissions of the League investigated the evils of the trade in opium and other drugs.

(iii) A statistical department provided reliable data of international interest. In these matters the League has no coercive powers, but it makes recommendations and gives publicity to abuses.

(e) The Geneva Protocol (1924)

The Powers again publicly renounced war and recognized the compulsory jurisdiction of the Permanent Court of International Justice at the Hague.

(f) Locarno Pact (1926)

Britain, France, Germany, Belgium, and Italy guaranteed the new frontiers set up in Europe by the Peace Treaties. Britain and Italy undertook to go to the assistance of any state in western Europe which suffered from any violation of this pledge, *i.e.*, to the help of France or Belgium if they were attacked by Germany.

(g) Kellogg Pact (1928)

This solemn agreement, subscribed to by all the Powers, was yet another undertaking to renounce war except in the case of self-defence.

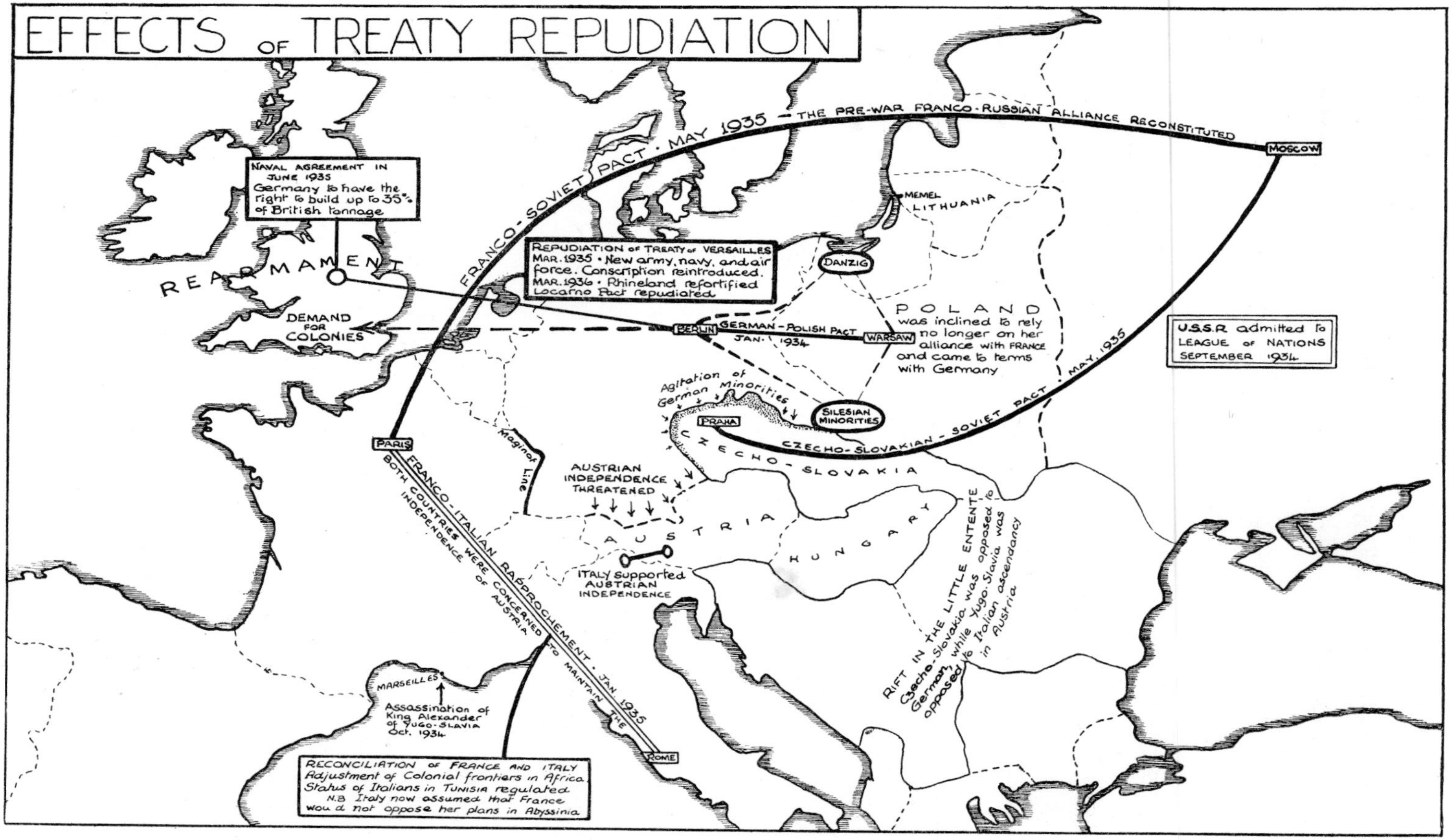

MAP 49

EFFECTS of TREATY REPUDIATION

THE PRE-WAR FRANCO-RUSSIAN ALLIANCE RECONSTITUTED

FRANCO - SOVIET PACT · MAY 1935

FRANCO - SOVIET PACT · MAY 1935

U.S.S.R admitted to
LEAGUE of NATIONS
SEPTEMBER 1934.

MEMEL

LITHUANIA

DANZIG

POLAND
was inclined to rely
no longer on her
alliance with France
and came to terms
with Germany

WARSAW

GERMAN - POLISH PACT
JAN. 1934.

BERLIN

Agitation of
German Minorities

SILESIAN
MINORITIES

PRAHA

CZECHO-SLOVAKIA

RIFT IN THE LITTLE ENTENTE
Czecho-Slovakia was opposed to
German, while Yugo-Slavia was
opposed to Italian ascendancy
in Austria.

H U N G A R Y

A U S T R I A

AUSTRIAN
INDEPENDENCE
THREATENED

ITALY supported
AUSTRIAN
INDEPENDENCE

REPUDIATION of TREATY of VERSAILLES
MAR. 1935 · New army, navy, and air
force. Conscription reintroduced.
MAR. 1936 · Rhineland refortified
Locarno Pact repudiated.

Maginot Line

PARIS

FRANCO - ITALIAN RAPPROCHEMENT · JAN 1935
BOTH COUNTRIES WERE CONCERNED TO MAINTAIN THE
INDEPENDENCE OF AUSTRIA.

ROME

MARSEILLES

Assassination of
King Alexander
Oct. 1934.

RECONCILIATION of FRANCE and ITALY
Adjustment of Colonial frontiers in Africa.
Status of Italians in Tunisia regulated.
N.B. Italy now assumed that France
would not oppose her plans in Abyssinia.

NAVAL AGREEMENT in
JUNE 1935
Germany to have the
right to build up to 35%
of British tonnage.

R E A R M A M E N T

DEMAND
for
COLONIES

MOSCOW

EFFECTS OF TREATY REPUDIATION

Map 49 suggests that the settlement made at Versailles has failed completely to satisfy the needs of Europe. Not only has the defeated state of Germany openly repudiated the restrictive clauses of the Treaty, but the victor states, recognizing that the collective security of the League Covenant is uncertain, have reverted to pre-War methods of forming alliances and piling up armaments. Two countries, Italy and Japan, have already undertaken military conquests in defiance of solemn treaty promises.

The main causes of this development have already been referred to on pp. 94 and 96 in connexion with the rise of Nazi Germany and the growth of militant Fascism under Mussolini in Italy.

The principal developments in addition to Hitler's repudiation of the Treaty of Versailles have been :

(a) *The* rapprochement *of France and Soviet Russia*

Overcoming their mutual dislike of each other's constitution, in much the same way as Imperial Russia and France came together in 1894 (see Map 1), the two Powers completed a new alliance in 1934.

(b) *The Rearmament of the Great Powers*

France, ever vigilant to guard her security, constructed a strong line of fortifications along her eastern frontier (the Maginot Line). Britain announced plans in 1937 of rearmament on a scale to make her the strongest Power in Europe. Russia postponed the completion of her second ' five-year plan ' in order to concentrate on the manufacture of munitions. The rulers of Italy and Germany not only increased their armaments, but also began to encourage in the minds of their people the idea that war was necessary, inevitable, and splendid.

(c) *Anglo-German Rivalry*

This disturbing feature of pre-War Europe has reappeared in the German demand for colonial territory.

EXERCISES

(1)

(i) Name the provinces A. When were they annexed by state Z ? Give two reasons for the opposition of state P.

(ii) When was island M united with Greece ? What statesman was responsible for this union ?

(iii) Of what race are the inhabitants of island N ? What power acquired control in 1912, and why was possession maintained ?

(iv) When were the boundaries YY superseded ? Explain why (a) country C was dissatisfied, and (b) country Z alarmed.

(v) Identify area B. When was it made an independent state, and why ?

(vi) Identify the towns E, F, G, H, and J. Mention some event of historical importance in the case of each one of them.

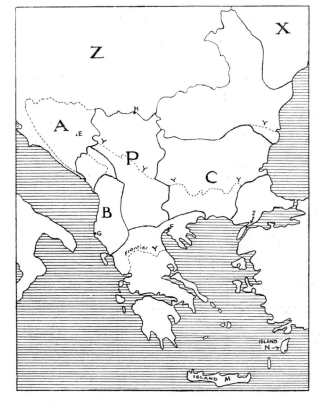

(2) On an outline-map of Europe and the Middle East :

(i) Shade the countries which joined the Central Powers, and write in each the date when they entered the War.

(ii) Insert a thick line to show (a) the western front, (b) the eastern front, (c) the Italian front, (d) the Armenian front, (e) the Salonika front, (f) the Mesopotamian front, (g) the Palestine front.

(iii) Show by arrows the Allied attempt to force the passage of the Straits, the Austrian victory at Caporetto, and the German thrust into Roumania.

(iv) Name the Allies that were crushed in 1915, 1916, and 1917 respectively.

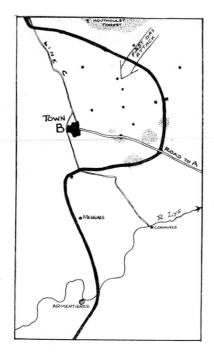

(3)

(i) Identify road A, town B, and line C.
(ii) Give date of (*a*) first German attack in this sector, (*b*) first gas attack, (*c*) great British offensive.
(iii) What natural features facilitated Allied defence north of this sector ?

(4) On an outline-map of Northern France insert and name :

(i) The Channel Ports.
(ii) Paris.
(iii) Verdun.

Shade the greatest area of German occupation and mark and name three decisive battles which stopped the German advance.

(5)

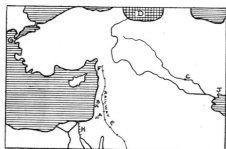

(i) Enumerate the Turkish war-fronts, and indicate them on the map.
(ii) Identify battles A and B and siege C.
(iii) Name the subject-people massacred at D and the Turkish railway E.
(iv) When were British forces engaged at F, G, H, and J ?

(6)

(i) Name states C, G, and H and their capitals.
(ii) Why did these three states make an alliance, and what was it called ?
(iii) Name the chief minorities in B and G.
(iv) For what reason were K and H unfriendly after the Great War.
(v) What were the internal and external difficulties of state C.
(vi) Which of all these states was most satisfied with the Peace Settlement ?

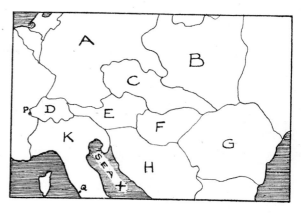

(7)

(i) On an outline-map of the Far East insert Korea, Manchuria, Jehol, Shantung Peninsula, Peiping, Canton, Nanking, Shanghai, Hong Kong.

(ii) What were the resources of Manchuria that attracted Japan?

(iii) What was the Kuo-Min-Tang party? Where were its headquarters?

(iv) What was the former name of Peiping, and who changed it?

(v) What is the strategic importance of Hong Kong?

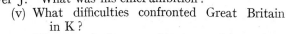

(8)

(i) Name territories A, B, C, D, and E. State who acquired these mandated areas.

(ii) What colonies did mandate A link together?

(iii) When did Great Britain withdraw from mandate over P?

(iv) Who was the post-War ruler over J. What was his chief ambition?

(v) What difficulties confronted Great Britain in K?

(vi) Who acquired a mandate over islands M? What type of a mandate was given?

(vii) What Powers feared the expansion of islands N?

(viii) Name port Q, and state its importance to Britain.

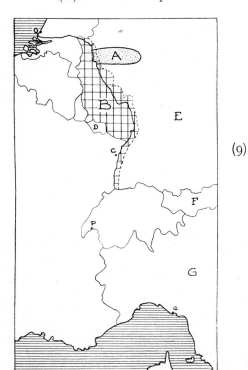

(9)

(i) Enumerate the evidence to show that this is a post-War map of Western Europe.

(ii) When did France invade area A?

(iii) What limitations were placed on Germany in area B?

(iv) Who acquired town C at the Peace Conference?

(v) Why was a plebiscite held in area D?

(vi) Name state E. Why did state F want to unite with state E?

(vii) Name towns O and P, and state their connexion with the League of Nations.

(viii) Name town Q. What important treaty was concluded in this town between state E and Soviet Russia?

(ix) Account for the decline of democracy in State G.

(10) On an outline-map of Europe :

   (i) Shade those countries which retained a democratic form of government in 1934.

   (ii) Insert the capitals Berlin, Rome, and Moscow. What circumstances made it possible for the rulers of these Governments to rise to power ?

   (iii) What benefits have these dictators conferred upon their subjects ?

   (iv) What do you understand by the " Rome-Berlin Axis " ?

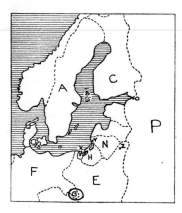

(11)

   (i) What states disputed the ownership of islands B, and by what authority was the quarrel settled ?

   (ii) Name states E and N, and give the reason for their dispute over town Z.

   (iii) Who ruled area H ? What provisions were made at the Peace Conference regarding port X ?

   (iv) What problems arose over town Y, and how were they settled ?

   (v) Why was a plebiscite held at G, and what was its result ?

   (vi) Give the three names of town O used before the War, during the War, and after the War respectively.

   (vii) Name the dictators of states E, F, and P in 1934.

INDEX

(B) = Battle   (T) = Treaty   (F) = Fortress

INDEX

I

INDEX

INDEX

INDEX